NETBALL—A TACTICAL APPROACH

NETBALL
A TACTICAL APPROACH

Sally Dewhurst-Hands

FABER AND FABER
London   Boston

First published in 1980
by Faber and Faber Limited
3 Queen Square London WC1N 3AU
Set by Latimer Trend & Company Ltd Plymouth
Printed in Great Britain by
Lowe & Brydone Ltd Thetford
All rights reserved

© *1980 by Sally Dewhurst-Hands*

CONDITIONS OF SALE

This book is sold subject to the condition that it shall not, by way of trade or otherwise, be lent, re-sold, hired out or otherwise circulated without the publisher's prior consent in any form of binding or cover other than that in which it is published and without a similar condition including this condition being imposed on the subsequent purchaser

British Library Cataloguing in Publication Data

Dewhurst-Hands, Sally
  Netball.
  1. Netball
  I. Title
  796.32   GV889.6   79-41501

  ISBN 0-571-11496-2
  ISBN 0-571-11542-x Pbk

Contents

1. Introduction	*page* 9
2. Tactics: A Broad View	12
3. Positional Responsibilities	16
4. Team Tactics	27
5. Attacking Tactics	40
6. Defending Tactics	65
Conclusion	85

Chapter 1
Introduction

It has become increasingly obvious that netball has achieved a secure place in the physical education curriculum and a favoured one. Equipment is minimal, the hard-surfaced playing area can be used in most weathers, needing little upkeep and attention, and the majority of secondary schools possess one or more courts on their own sites. In addition, and possibly because of the points mentioned above, research investigations have shown that it is a widely practised game with secondary schoolgirls and comes high on the list of preferred activities.

From enquiry, it would seem that the game's popularity is not restricted to the school. Socially there appears to be an increase in the time available for pursuing leisure activities, and of necessity local authorities have begun to recognize the need to increase recreational facilities to satisfy public demand. Many large industrial firms are providing sports grounds for their employees and in some instances giving time for play. This extension of existing facilities and the increase in time available, together with the need of women to participate in some form of physical recreation, have resulted in netball clubs becoming a reality and not merely, as in the recent past, a desirable goal for the future. Once again the minimal equipment needed and the fact that the game embraces all shapes, sizes and ages recommends it as a 'come back' sport for many.

Undoubtedly the skills of players at all levels have improved greatly in recent years; schoolgirls, club or county players and internationals alike are all displaying skills of an increasingly high standard. Much time and energy is devoted to their development and the result can certainly be observed in a marked improvement in play.

Much as one acknowledges the importance of skill development, however, the full potential of the game will never be achieved if further thought and consideration are not given to the more cognitive area of play—that of tactics. Little if any literature exists which deals exclusively with this aspect of the game; the publications currently in circulation are heavily slanted toward the individual and her personal problems regarding the acquisition of the skills of the game.

There may, of course, be very obvious reasons for this. On the one hand, skills may be regarded as the first priority, since one school of thought proposes that the application of tactical knowledge requires a relatively high level of playing ability. On the other hand, the reason may be concerned with rule changes. In any game it is these that form and provide a framework around which tactics are constructed. The rules of netball not only appear to change relatively frequently compared with those of other games but also affect the game so drastically that people may well have been wary of committing themselves to print when the results could be outdated before publication. Perhaps a more realistic reason for the dearth of literature on tactics might be that tactical theories are merely considered personal opinions and few have had the courage or conviction to propose concrete suggestions as to how the game could or should be played strategically. One would have to include suggestions on how the skills might be applied in the game so that a team might combine its strengths to advantage, disguise its weaknesses and exploit the opposition. To make such thoughts or beliefs explicit unquestionably exposes one to criticism. Most people concerned with the game, whether player, teacher or coach, have some feelings as to how best the game should be structured; and when one is concerned with a subjective matter of opinion, measuring success becomes extremely difficult. One opinion, however much opposed to or distinct from another, may be equally valid—and who is to judge?

Nevertheless it is my belief that tactical thinkers, including teachers, coaches and players, will welcome a book which attempts to deal systematically with tactics. Whether it stimulates discussion or initiates debate it will at least provide a pivot around which thinking can revolve. The present lack of any literary referential focus forces both coaches and players to revert to stereotyped traditional views on tactics—undoubtedly valuable, but restricting if not structured for the modern game. The limitations inherent in this somewhat backward-looking practice are obvious—tactically, the game for the vast majority will stagnate.

It is this apparent neglect of a most crucial aspect of play and its resulting inhibiting effect on the game which has motivated me to attempt to clarify my own thoughts on the subject, and in the process produce a statement on tactics which I hope will serve to stimulate others to re-examine their own theories as well as to challenge mine.

Chapter 2
Tactics: A Broad View

It might prove interesting at this juncture to look briefly at a few tactical principles which affect netball and which should have interesting bearings on many games. To explain this, it is necessary to clarify the meaning of tactics; and I have interpreted tactics as *the strategic planning of a course of action with a view to gaining advantage by outwitting the opposition.* Methods adopted are usually well practised and often result in scoring goals or points while at the same time preventing the opposition achieving the same end.

I propose that a team of players who are employing a tactical approach and are tactically aware will gain advantage since they:
 a. produce a united effort where playing responsibility is distributed which will ultimately result in economy of individual effort;
 b. present problems to the opposition;
 c. more quickly adjust and solve those problems posed by the opposing side.

The logical outcome of the above points suggests that if the skill factor is negated by equality being established between two teams, then the effective application of tactics must be decisive in ultimate success. It is also believed by some that a good tactician or tactically minded team will often gain supremacy over more highly skilled players. This is no doubt a debatable point and other factors may well have to be taken into account; nevertheless it is a belief held by many top-class players.

One point which needs mentioning is that of the skill level appropriate to the tactics being employed. It must be acknowledged that the lower the level of skill, the more frequently will chance happenings occur that are haphazard and unplanned. With the increase of skill, players become more able to give time to and focus attention on the understanding and application of planned strategies. It must of course be left to teachers and coaches, and eventually to the individual player herself, to select tactics appropriate to the skill standard of those involved and to decide, when the practice of a certain tactic breaks down, whether this is due entirely or partially to lack of playing ability or to the strategy itself.

When dealing in general with tactics as they apply to many games, two factors which regularly occur, and which are often related considerations, are *space* and *time*. Whether in defence or attack an awareness of and concern for both are of specific significance for the tactically minded player or coach.

SPACE

Any team on the attack will constantly be aware of the need to make or create space into which free players may move; the greater the space the more room there will be for manoeuvrability and adjustment, thus allowing for a greater margin of error. The greater the space a player has in which to move, the freer she is in terms of action; her stroke, drive or throw will be unimpeded, and provided she also has the time this can be completed with the minimum of interference. Attacking players must be concerned with filling space, as distinct from congesting space, for the spatial limitations imposed by the rules call for acute awareness of width and depth. Defending players should no less cultivate a spatial awareness so that they can orientate themselves positively towards, for example, lines, posts, the ball and other players—their opponents or their own side. Accuracy in terms of assessment of relative distances should become an integral part of the defence skill, since it is their responsibility to minimize the space into which the opponents may move, and if possible to defend so closely that players cannot be used, thus reducing the number of choices offered. Defences must see their role as taking away space from the opposition as well as being concerned with covering or guarding space—as in zone defence, where the emphasis is on the space and not the player.

As a result of this spatial awareness, the movement and positioning of a good defending player may well achieve success by:
  a. eliminating her opponent;
  b. forcing the player with the ball to alter her decision;
  c. causing the ball to be played out of court.

Generally speaking by reducing choice or forcing a skill breakdown the defending player should gain an advantage.

In games where space is not shared, for example tennis, cricket and rounders, this problem may not arise, for the nature of these games differs in so far as territory is not invaded and the movements of defending players affect only the spaces available into which the ball may be played. Although this may well influence decisions the actions themselves are not impeded.

TIME

The nature of the game suggests that the question of time be given priority, for as well as the spatial demands the players face the challenge imposed by the three-second rule. A team is concerned with time because for every action, time is required and, although the amounts will vary in degree, the fact remains that any action takes time to complete. If time is afforded a player, either by her own efforts or those of others on her own side, she has the maximum opportunity to produce an appropriate action, which will have a good chance of being successful. If time is *taken* from the player by the opponents then she may well be forced to hurry or rush a shot or pass which, because of its hasty execution, may be technically inefficient and fail to achieve its objective.

A further point to be taken into account is that time is needed for decisions to be made, and the more effective the defence is in taking time, the more likely they are to force a wrong decision or to encourage a state of indecision.

A concern for rhythm is important in both attack and defence; a defending team can, for example, employ a tactic which involves breaking or interfering with the rhythm of the opposition, whilst an attacking team can vary their rhythm in an attempt to outwit. The ability to slow the pace of a game or to accelerate it is sometimes the determining factor in establishing supremacy.

Finally time can be used when, for example, at a critical moment in a game a team plays the ball with the sole objective of filling time or, as some prefer to talk of it, wasting time.

The time factor is an important consideration in any tactical plan; a team on the attack should manoeuvre to provide themselves with adequate time, whereas a defending team should aim to take time away from their opponents thereby forcing errors, adversely affecting decision-making, as well as skill.

Before leaving this rather general chapter it should be emphasized yet again just how influential are the space–time requirements to the very nature of the game. The fact that a ball may be held for three seconds only demands that preparation, timing of moves and recoveries be speedy and accurate, for when mistakes are made corrections are always very difficult and often impossible.

The restriction of playing areas adds a dimension to netball not seen in other games and the discipline called for by these two factors characterizes and distinguishes the game from all others.

Chapter 3
Positional Responsibilities

Before defining the specific responsibilities of each playing position, it might prove useful to outline the thinking which brought about these distinctions. This should help the reader to see the playing roles in relation to the game as a whole, and to appreciate that a basic premise needs to be grasped before any progressive tactics may evolve.

One distinctive feature of netball which should determine much of the tactical thinking in the game is that playing areas are severely restricted, and these restrictions, unlike those imposed in other games, are specific to each player. In the racket games, for example, the net limits the playing area, but this is a restriction which applies to all players alike; while in field games such as hockey, lacrosse and soccer there are also restrictions imposed by the rules regarding playing areas but here, too, they are common to all. In this respect netball falls into a category of its own, for the spatial freedom of each player is clearly defined in the rules governing play; and the restrictions placed, for example, on a Goal Attack and a Goal Defence are significantly different from those placed on the two Centres, though some territory is common to all four players. The uniqueness of the game in this respect makes it crucial that tactics be employed to ensure that despite each player's spatial restrictions she is able to make a maximum contribution. For this to happen, tactical decisions must be structured in relation to each individual playing area and the player's specific role.

It must not be assumed, however, that a player, having clarified her particular responsibility and therefore her role, remains permanently within these confines for the duration of any one game. If this were the case the challenge of the game would inevitably be diminished, resulting in a recognized, repetitive pattern of play, readily distinguishable and boring for both players and spectators alike.

PLAYING RESPONSIBILITIES

In any team game one of the aims is the unifying of a group of people who then proceed as one co-operative body to attempt to outwit and outplay their opponents. For this to happen it seems only good sense that each member of the group takes an equal responsibility and makes her contribution to the whole.

If this simple idea is accepted then the question that may well be asked is how do seven players make a consistent and maximum contribution? It is more often the rule than the exception to see in schoolgirl netball, and indeed in club and county games too, players who, with the best possible intentions, find their efforts thwarted and the game culminating in confusion, congestion and general chaos. This predicament is common in games of all standards and all types and leads one to examine why, when all seven players appear to be making a major effort, the overall result remains ineffective.

The main reason would seem to be in most cases that individuals fail to recognize the responsibilities specific to their position, and in this ignorance take on other players' duties and neglect their own. It is not suggested that there should be no interchange of responsibilities, but this presupposes first, an awareness of particular roles and second, a group awareness of any exchanges which might be made; changes cannot be made by individual players in isolation without causing confusion. It is crucial that players recognize positional requirements and grasp the connection between their particular role and that of the two others with whom they must be able to relate. These relationships will be explained and discussed in detail in the next chapter.

Basic security comes only through a thorough knowledge of one's own positional demands, and the security of a team arises as a result of confident transfer of responsibilities.

Each player has quite distinct priorities in terms of her commitment to the rest of the team and these are as follows:

Goal Shooter

Her role is to *score goals* not simply to 'shoot' or 'try to score'. She carries a heavy responsibility, for without her accuracy the efforts of the rest of the team will go unrewarded. In her restricted playing area it is vital that she be agile, alert and adept at sudden changes of direction. Much of her work in freeing herself so that she may receive the ball in the circle depends to a large extent on her consistency in shooting from anywhere; this includes being able to win rebounds should Goal Attack shoot and miss. A really accurate shooter has the complete freedom of the attacking circle because she can afford to receive the ball in any position. This knowledge gives her and the feeding players a confidence and security which in turn enlarges the possibilities of tactical supremacy. A shooter limited to a shooting radius of three or four feet increases the responsibility of the feeds by restricting the playing area; she makes her own job more difficult by making her movements to some extent predictable and therefore more easily defended, and she often inhibits the Goal Attack by commandeering an area of the court and consequently congesting the already small shooting zone. Often a Goal Shooter's position, one that may so easily be star-studded, deteriorates into a monotonous pattern of play around the goal post, restricted in movement, and devoid of vitality. The authority this prime attacking player should have is transferred to the feeders, leaving the Goal Shooter a mere recipient; the other players find the added responsibility outside the limits of their personal brief.

Goal Attack

The position of Goal Attack is one which leaves itself exposed both to criticism and praise; and it is only on analysis that one begins to understand the enormous demands made upon this player. As one of the two shooters, the Goal Attack's prime concern is the scoring of goals and she must at all times consider this her main priority. However, her playing area is much greater than that of the Goal Shooter and this in itself can be physically taxing. Often she receives the ball whilst travelling at a considerable speed and, although I don't want to be diverted into the details of skill requirements, it is sufficient to say that this is exacting, especially when a shot is to follow.

A Goal Attack must balance her play so that on the one hand, she is able to score goals and on the other, she can make a contribution as a feed, decoy and initiator in the attacking third. Such a dual responsibility asks much of a player and many fail by emphasizing one aspect at the expense of the other. It is not uncommon to find a Goal Attack working very hard in the attacking third of the court, but in doing so she often inhibits the Wing Attack, crowds the area and leaves herself too weary to score.

Wing Attack

The demands made on a Wing Attack may appear simple, but in fact they are taxing and complex. It is an attractive playing position, as the majority of the work is executed around the scoring area; it offers scope for dynamism, skill and speed and it needs variety of passing in addition to intelligent scheming, and appropriate decision-making.

A skilled player recognizes the importance of her role as the main feeder of the shooters and that the job is incomplete until the shooters have successfully converted a shot into a goal. This latter point emphasizes the fact that the Wing Attack's responsibility lies not merely in feeding the shooters but feeding the shooters in the circle; and that even at this juncture she may well be called upon to support the circle players who may decide to pass in order to reposition themselves more advantageously before attempting a shot.

It may well be that on certain occasions the Wing Attack initiates a pass out from the circle when she reads the game more clearly than the shooter in possession of the ball; there might be a short Goal Attack, for example, who is being forced to shoot from the edge of the circle and is defended by a tall Goal Defence. (Fig. 1)

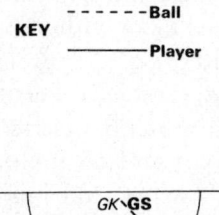

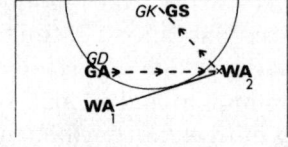

Fig. 1 Wing Attack initiates a pass from Goal Attack by sprinting and indicating, she then feeds the more favourably positioned Goal Shooter. Straight line indicates path of player and dotted line that of ball.

Secondary to this feeding role a Wing Attack, in conjunction with the Centre, is needed to ensure the safe passage of the ball from the centre third into the predominantly offensive area, the attacking third. An intelligent player is constantly adjusting and, with the other attacking players, scheming for openings; she is continually orientating herself and her moves so that she is for the majority of the time in close proximity to the attacking area—her main field of play.

Centre

Many of the requirements of this position are inherent in the name itself. In a sense the position is a diverse one in that there is a need for equal contribution in both attack and defence, whilst at the same time she is the major link in uniting the attacking and defending areas. With the licence afforded by this flexibility a Centre has to be self-disciplined, for this width of responsibility clearly indicates that too much effort in attack will inevitably be at the expense of work in defence and vice versa.

The Centre is probably the only player in a position to assess the 'flavour' of a game since she is an integral part of the whole and has the opportunity to ascertain a comprehensive view of play. This privilege presents her with further responsibilities for she must take the initiative in directing routes of attack as well as controlling the speed of play, and whilst initiating these moves must also be involved in the outcome. It will therefore be obvious that her contribution must be a balanced one otherwise she will find that she is in no position to read the game and as a result will not be in a position to dictate appropriate tactical play.

Wing Defence

An effective Wing Defence is frequently an unnoticed player, unobtrusive but by no means negative. Her position demands tremendous powers of concentration, the ability to react quickly, an intuitive and perceptive mind and the ability to make prompt yet accurate decisions. Her prime role is that of defence and her concentration must be focused on her opponent, the Wing Attack.

To prevent the Wing Attack, the key feed player, gaining possession of the ball, particularly in the attacking third, the Wing Defence must be self-disciplined. She should be dogged in her determination to shadow her opponent for the majority of the game. She should recognize the potential danger of her failure to do so and ignore the temptation to share in the limelight often enjoyed by the attacking players.

As with all defensive positions a Wing Defence's job is a difficult one in so far as most of her actions take place in relation to her opponent. She is on the whole a reactor and not a prime mover, and diligence is vital for this position. One might be tempted to suggest that a competent and effective Wing Defence, in a skilled game, may handle the ball little but neither will her opponent, the Wing Attack; while in a game involving less skill the result of her industry may become evident in her increased involvement.

In addition to her defending role she has to co-operate with other defending players and with the Centre in order to get the ball safely out of the defending half of the court before resuming her role as 'watch dog'.

Goal Defence

The position of Goal Defence is a dangerously exciting one because of its proximity to the opponents' goal; exhilarating because of the scope it offers for anticipation and intuition, it requires a player to be disciplined and highly skilled.

The prime responsibility of a Goal Defence is that of preventing her opponent receiving the ball in the circle, the area from which a score may be registered. This must be her first priority and all her movements, thoughts and decisions should be made with this one objective in mind.

Like the Goal Keeper and Wing Defence, the Goal Defence as a defending player has the distinction of being a reactor and not an initiator; this requires a positional awareness that leads to immediacy of action. The significance of this is illustrated by the fact that she must at all times be aware of her position in relation to the goal, her opponent and to the lines bounding the court. It is only through this awareness that she can make accurate and speedy decisions in a limited area.

Although she is initially concerned with defending, she may well be called upon to contribute in a secondary capacity to assist the Wing Defence and the Goal Keeper in easing the pressure in the goal third by safely transporting the ball from the goal third into the centre third.

Goal Keeper

The positional naming of this player is self-explanatory. The responsibility of the Goal Keeper is to guard or defend the goal, the final objective of the opposition's manoeuvres and tactics.

In order to satisfy this requirement the Goal Keeper needs a singleness of mind, for as the ultimate defending player an error on her part usually culminates in, at best, possession of the ball in the circle, or, at worst, a goal.

The tactics adopted by the Goal Keeper are influenced greatly by those employed by the Goal Shooter; to prevent this player gaining possession of the ball in the circle is her first priority. The strictest self-discipline is needed in conjunction with diligence and doggedness. A Goal Keeper cannot afford to make a mistake.

SUMMARY

Goal Shooter

Responsibility
1. To score goals.

Weaknesses
1. Insufficiently accurate.
2. Insufficiently versatile, so weak in tactical positioning.
3. Occasionally undertakes the feed responsibilities of Goal Attack and Wing Attack instead of being the main receiver of the ball in the circle.
4. Often, in preserving her composure for shooting, limits her play to the goal post area, thereby restricting herself and limiting the possible avenues for feeding.

Goal Attack

Responsibility
1. To score goals.
2. To help, discriminately, Wing Attack feed the circle.

Weaknesses
1. Insufficiently accurate.
2. Overplays her secondary role as feeder at the expense of her first priority of scoring goals.
3. Poaches and confuses Wing Attack's territory.

Wing Attack

Responsibility
1. To feed the shooters in the circle.

2. To ensure with Centre the safe passage of the ball from the centre third into the attacking third; and with the assistance of Goal Attack to feed the circle.

Weaknesses
1. Fails to make all moves positively orientated towards the circle and circle players.
2. Lacks variety in feeding circle players in the circle, so becoming predictable and easily countered.

Centre

Responsibility
1. To link the attacking and defending halves.
2. To contribute equally and discreetly in both areas.
3. To assess the game and initiate appropriate tactical response.

Weaknesses
1. Is unable to make equal contributions in both defence and attack.
2. Poor positioning and consequent breakdown of her linking role.
3. Makes too much effort in attack: congests the attacking third, eliminates Wing Attack and leaves a gap in the centre third.
4. Makes too much effort in defence: confuses Wing Defence, leaves a gap in the middle and leaves the attacking third weak.

Wing Defence

Responsibility
1. To prevent Wing Attack receiving the ball.
2. With Goal Defence or Centre, to ensure the safe passage of the ball from the defending half into the attacking half of the court.

Weaknesses
1. Has a tendency to leave Wing Attack too soon and give her attention to the ball.
2. Contributes too much in centre court attacking play—neglecting her major role: defending.
3. Doesn't always assess the defending third situation accurately, consequently withholding or congesting.

Goal Defence

Responsibility
1. To prevent the Goal Attack receiving the ball in the circle.
2. To assist the Wing Defence and Goal Keeper in passing the ball safely out of the defending third.

Weaknesses
1. Does not really defend closely enough.
2. Occasionally lacks composure and makes hasty decisions at critical moments.
3. Tends to indulge herself as a spare centre-court player.

Goal Keeper

Responsibility
1. To prevent the Goal Shooter receiving the ball in the circle.
2. To be available when called upon to assist with the safe passage of the ball from the circle area.

Weaknesses
1. Not sufficiently single-minded.
2. As involvement can be variable, i.e. in a one-sided game, not always ready to give maximum effort when required.
3. Doesn't look and see often enough.

To make a very long list of the requirements of each playing position would not be too difficult, but it is hoped that by being selective the point will be made that players are capable of only a certain amount, and it is important to discriminate between necessity and possibility: for absolute efficiency is the goal.

It is because of this that each playing role has been carefully analysed and only the essentials have been highlighted. For example, the Goal Shooter's job is seen to be a goal scorer not a recoverer of missed shots, a circle feed, or a decoy, all of which she may be asked to do but primarily she is required to score goals. Individuals must develop personal skills and bring them to their game, but if essential positional requirements can be mastered through positive tactical thinking then the maturation of players' tactical achievements will follow naturally.

Chapter 4
Team Tactics

In considering the build-up of team tactics, the necessity for the group to function as a whole unit seems obvious, but such a campaign is often a major stumbling block to the would-be coach. Frequently the problem lies in knowing where to start and, having started, how to proceed. I hope that the following suggestions may serve as pointers to what are seen to be elementary yet very essential 'understandings' if team tactics are to be employed with any effect.

1. Each player should be familiar with her own position, in practical terms; she should be fully aware of her responsibilities in that position, and must be sufficiently disciplined to accept the opportunities and limitations the position gives her.
2. Each player should understand the role of all other players and be particularly aware of the two players on either side of her: so, Centre is familiar with the work of both Wing Attack and Wing Defence, Goal Attack with Wing Attack and Goal Shooter, etc.
3. Each player should be fully aware of the need for team effort and not of a solo performance.

There are obvious questions arising from these points. How does a coach make her players aware of their particular responsibilities? How does she help the team present a united effort? How does she instil self-discipline into each team member?

There are no simple answers, and many coaches fail at this juncture for it is not sufficient merely to inform players of their roles; somehow players have to be trained to look, see and think. It is the application of knowledge at the right time and in the right place which ultimately brings success. Correct methods will produce reactions apparently spontaneously while the game is in progress, and coaching from the side-line is superfluous.

One way in which players can learn is by being exposed to many varied situations, which will probably occur during a game. These experiences serve to familiarize players with likely problems and to give them time during practice to exercise improvisation. The familiarity which this type of practice brings leads naturally to a confidence which in turn enhances play.

Tactics may only be utilized to the full when built on a proven foundation, and the following are methods which I have systematically selected and exploited over a period of many years, which for me have proved most successful.

BASIC CHAIN LINK

Whilst appreciating that there will always be situations arising that are specific to the occasion, the spatial peculiarities of the game suggest that if a player is restricted to territory A, unless she actively plays the ball in that area she will not make a contribution other than by acting as a decoy or by making space available for another player. (Fig. 2)

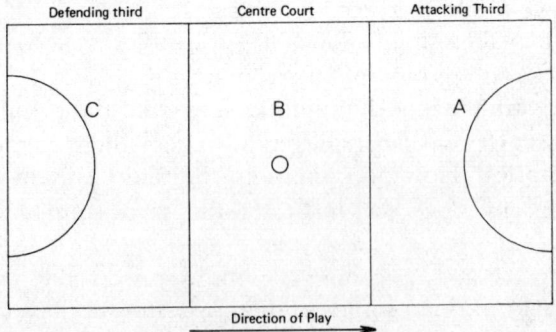

Fig: 2 Diagram to show the three areas of play: defending third, attacking third and centre court. Arrow shows direction of play

So it is a useful practice when thinking tactics to help players familiarize themselves with the depth and width of their playing areas. This can be encouraged by dividing the court into seven strips (if necessary with chalk). Each player receives and passes the ball within her appropriate area. Unless the width of the court is used seven passes will be very difficult. (Fig. 3)

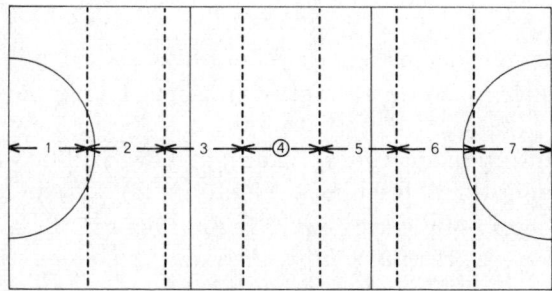

Fig. 3 Intensive court restrictions to help players recognize the width and depth of their playing areas

The ball travels from 1 to 7 and back from 7 to 1 many times, the players always remaining in their respective territories. As they become more efficient they should be encouraged to time their moves in relation to the previous receiver (essential for sound tactical play) and to utilize a variety of passing skills according to the distances over which the ball must be played, e.g. underarm, chest pass, shoulder pass, etc.

When this practice becomes reasonably efficient—and it may be surprising how long this can take—it can be developed so that players start outside their own territory but always receive the ball in it. Having successfully caught and passed the ball they must then assess the situation and re-position accordingly. This constant adjustment is the first stage in encouraging players to look and think.

A further development of this practice is for the players to choose to start either in or out of their territory, but continue to receive in their specific areas.

Finally, the effectiveness should be tested by the introduction of an opposition.

SUMMARY

1. Strip the court widthwise.
2. The ball is passed up and down the court with little movement by the players: the ball is handled in their own playing area.
3. The players stay in their area concentrating on familiarizing themselves with depth and width, i.e. playing the ball in every possible spot.
4. Concentration on timing whilst playing within the area (receiving the ball while accelerating, not slowing down).
5. Starting out of the area, receiving in the area.
6. Starting out, receiving in, with timing a major consideration.
7. Starting in or out—but receiving in.
8. Starting as the individual so chooses—receiving in but with opposition.

These somewhat rigid restrictions adequately serve many purposes: they discipline players but do not inhibit them; they encourage players to look and think; they demand a concern for timing; they encourage versatility in dodging and passing skills; they automatically provide a depth and width to the court, for every area is always fed by one player.

This basic chain link (as it is commonly known) can serve as a basis for most structural planning, and when players recognize its value and are sufficiently competent to progress, many exciting variations may be introduced.

Variation 1: Reversing Roles

If for any reason Goal Attack is not free to receive the ball from Wing Attack, Goal Shooter should free herself in Goal Attack's territory—so taking on the role of Goal Attack. Observing this interchange, Goal Attack leaves her own territory and attempts to receive the next pass in Goal Shooter's area; in this way, the roles of Goal Attack and Goal Shooter are reversed. (Figs. 4 and 5)

It is important to note that in reversing the roles the two players concerned need to recognize their different playing areas and adjust accordingly so as to ensure that each area is provided for and no one area is congested.

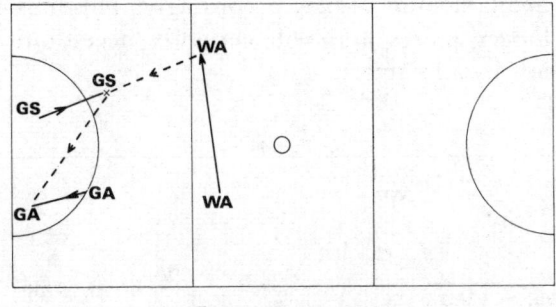

Fig. 4 Goal Shooter and Goal Attack roles reversed

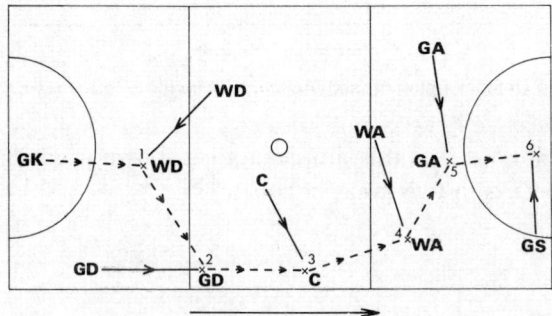

Fig. 5 Wing Defence and Goal Defence roles reversed

Variation 2: Missing a Player

It may be that in a similar situation the ball is passed successfully from Goal Keeper to Goal Defence, that Wing Defence is marked and Centre, the next player in the basic link, adjusts to take the role of Wing Defence, but instead of reversing roles as in Fig. 5, the situation may suggest that one player be missed completely. (Fig. 6)

In this example it would be the player taking on the role of Centre who would be omitted, for Centre has moved into the Wing Defence's playing territory. Instead of attempting to reverse roles with the Centre, Wing Defence keeps the space clear for the attacking players to adjust to the additional depth of court available and to play accordingly. This may involve slightly longer passes and will certainly necessitate spatial adjustments by all players.

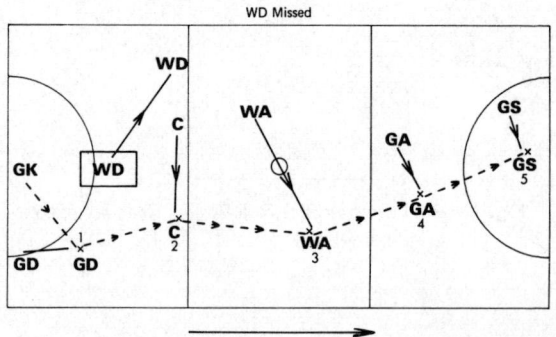

Fig. 6 Wing Defence being missed. Adjustments made by other team members

A development on this simple tactic is shown when reversing of roles occurs in two areas of court. (Fig. 7)

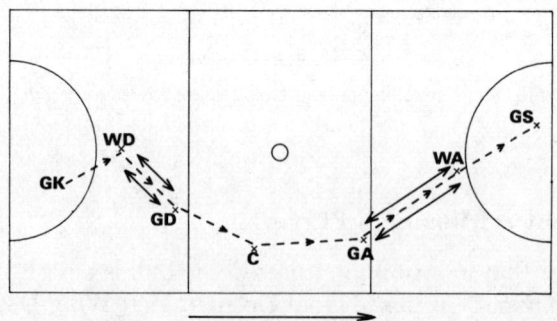

Fig. 7 Reversing of Wing Defence and Goal Defence, and Wing Attack and Goal Attack

Variation 3: Reversing and Missing

A further development may occur when both reversing and missing are combined in one passing sequence. (Fig. 8)

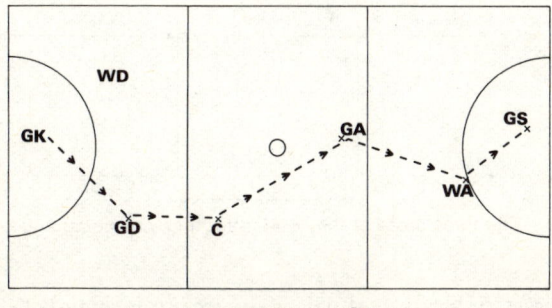

Fig. 8 Reversing and missing: Wing Defence missed; Goal Attack and Wing Attack reversed

It must be emphasized that these variations on the basic chain link should *not* be attempted until there is absolute security within the link itself, for undoubtedly confusion and disillusionment will result.

It seems worth pointing out that many teams do reverse playing roles, miss out links, etc., but this is usually done spontaneously and seldom at a conscious level, so that players rarely make the adjustments demanded by the situations. It is imperative that for tactical efficiency all actions and counter actions be performed at a conscious level because it is only then that all seven team members can present a united front and work as a team.

Growing from the idea that each playing area on the court should be served by one player, more advanced tactics can be considered by dividing the court into thirds instead of seven strips. By the very nature of the playing positions the court readily divides itself into three distinct areas—attacking, defending, and centre or linking areas. (Fig. 9)

There are three players who are directly responsible for each area. (Wing Attack and Wing Defence being the overlap—see

34 Team Tactics

section on positional responsibilities.) The tactics of any one area may be applied to those of the other two.

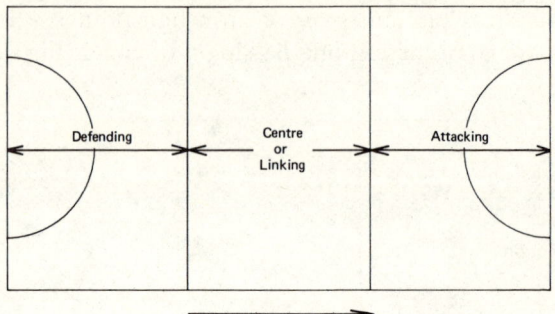

Fig. 9 The three areas of the court: attacking, defending and centre

Using the defending third as an example it will be appreciated that the job of the three players involved—Wing Defence, Goal Keeper and Goal Defence—is to secure the safe passage of the ball from the defending third into the centre third.

A reasonable assumption may be that if players are favourably positioned the basic chain link could be played. However, in many situations players are adjusting from defending roles to those initiating attacking play, and inevitably certain decisions and subsequent actions must be taken in accordance with the state of play. The actions taken can be conscious and deliberate, if the three players work together as a sub-unit within the team unit.

It must first be established that the three players concerned will keep working until the ball is safely in the centre third. No other player will interfere and the responsibility rests entirely with them. However simple this may appear, its value in terms of security, information and total team understanding is remarkable for:

    a. it gives all players an indication as to when they are expected to play the ball—the idea of duration and participation (this does not mean that attacking players do not participate, for every player should be repositioning and preparing);

b. it makes the trio aware of each other;
c. it gives the trio a relatively clear area to work in;
d. it encourages a concern for spatial awareness;
e. all players know what is actually happening.

The playing of the ball can follow one of many variations, but what must be clearly understood is that any one player may be called upon to play any one of three roles.

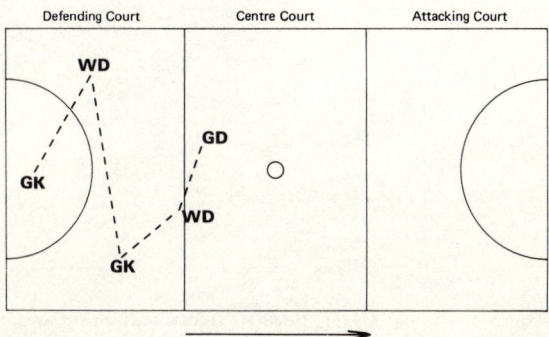

Fig. 10 The defending trio are responsible for the safe passage of the ball out of the defending court

This demands acute awareness as players are switching in and out of others' positions, interchanging, adjusting and re-adjusting, all within a very short space of time and within a limited playing area. To attempt this type of interchange players must look, assess and act accordingly; individuals cannot work in isolation. It is a group effort which must be shared and fully understood by all.

Remembering that each third of the court is served by three players and that each unit of three caters for the covering, yet not the congestion, of its particular area, it is a useful practice to encourage spatial and positional awareness. (Fig. 11)

In Fig. 11, the numbers denote the territory and the letters the players. The object of the practice is to keep the ball moving, from territory to territory, players continually adjusting, so that each territory is always provided for yet never congested. It can be seen that if player B receives the ball in territory 2 she is playing as Goal Defence whereas if she plays it in 3 she

36 Team Tactics

is acting as Wing Defence. It is worth noting that in a match, should player A, i.e. Goal Keeper, receive the ball in territory 3 thus taking on the role of Wing Defence, her territorial limitations (imparted by the rules) will not permit her to complete the job of Wing Defence; therefore the other two players must recognize and adjust to the situation.

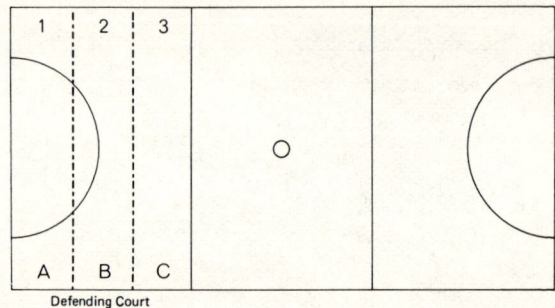

Fig. 11 A practice to help players develop spatial and group awareness: the ball is passed from 1 to 2 to 3 to 3 to 2 to 1

Similar principles may be applied to the centre court and attacking trios, the object being that each third of the court is always adequately served by three players. If, for example, in the centre court the basic chain link is successfully being implemented then, in Fig. 12a below, Wing Defence would play the ball in territory A, Centre in B and Wing Attack in C.

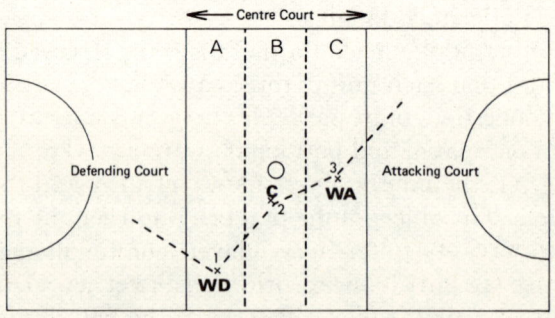

Fig. 12a Basic chain working smoothly

Team Tactics 37

However, should the situation arise when Centre has to receive the ball in A (Fig. 12b), she then takes the role of Wing Defence and the other two centre court players take on the jobs of Centre and Wing Attack.

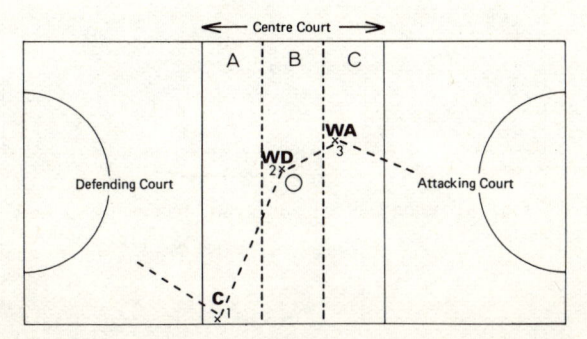

Fig. 12b Centre and Wing Defence deliberately changing roles

In the attacking court the principles involved are exactly the same. In short, a concentrated awareness is necessary within a limited space involving the close co-operation of three players. There is the need for flexibility, for intelligent reading of the situation, and for the players to act confidently, positively, and with complete understanding. Figs. 13–17 show possible examples of deliberate adjustments by the various trios.

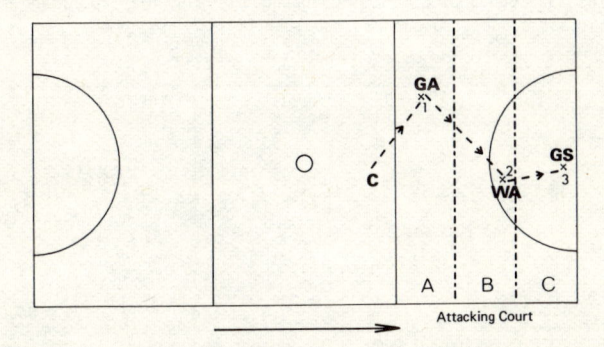

Fig. 13 Wing Attack and Goal Attack consciously reverse roles

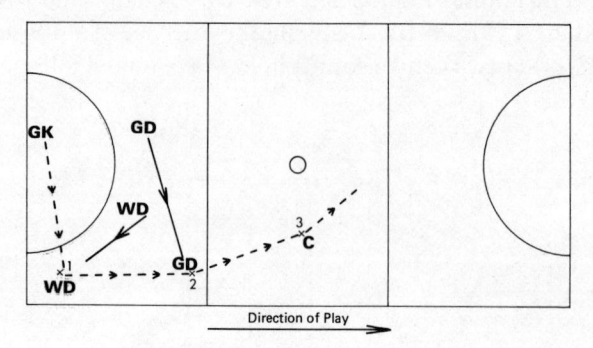

Fig. 14 Wing Defence and Goal Defence reverse roles

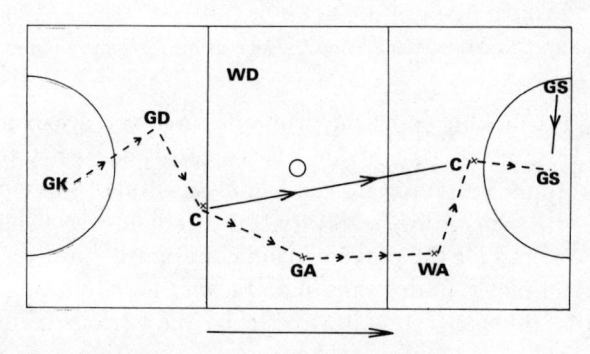

Fig. 15 Wing Defence being missed, the other team members adjust

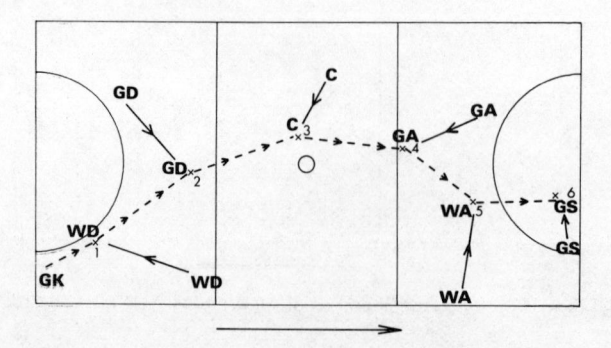

Fig. 16 Reversing of Wing Defence and Goal Defence and Wing Attack and Goal Attack

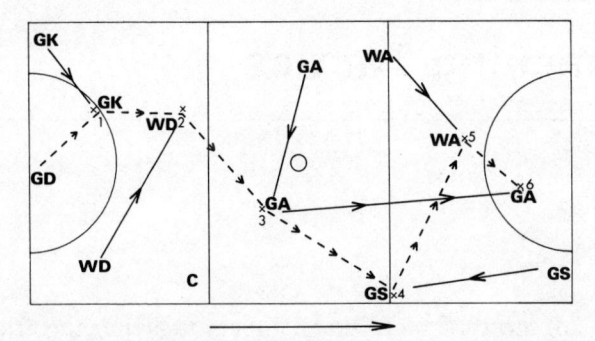

Fig. 17 A further development occurs when reversing and missing are combined in one passing sequence: Goal Keeper and Goal Defence reverse; Centre is missed; Goal Shooter takes the role of Wing Attack and Goal Attack becomes Goal Shooter. Goal Attack and Wing Attack reversed

Chapter 5
Attacking Tactics

There are certain factors which appear to favour the attacking team, and while recognition of these by both sides will give equal knowledge, the advantage should nevertheless remain with the team in possession of the ball for:
1. Within the limits of the rules, they may select where they will position themselves on court (how best this can be used to advantage will be discussed later).
2. The attackers have the right to initiate movement. This is a tremendous advantage for as prime movers they make their own time, decide on their own space and force the defenders into assuming the role of reactors.
3. If so desired, they may choose to follow a predetermined plan which usually leads to quicker decisions and slicker passing.

Before proposing possible tactics it may prove valuable to discuss methods currently practised, and in so doing suggest their weaknesses and limitations. The easiest place to start would be at the centre as the majority of tactics affecting attacking play seem to be influenced in some way by the centre pass.

CENTRE PASS BODY SIGNS

Most readers will be familiar with the teams which relate their centre passes to body signs; these are signs made by Centre before each pass: for example, two feet together indicate Wing Attack or one hand on the hip Goal Defence, and so on. It might be argued that this method has been relatively successful

over the years, and that many teams have enjoyed a limited success as a result of it. Unfortunately it falls down on two counts:
1. Centre is asked to remember the signs and the appropriate players.
2. The method can produce too much anxiety, for the players are asked to see, and translate and then commit themselves regardless of what ensues. Doubts will arise when the sign is not obvious, and undoubtedly confusion, should the sign be misinterpreted.

There are teams which adopt a word such as 'rubber' or 'kettle', when each player permitted into the centre third identifies herself with a letter and takes the centre pass in rotation. So: R = Goal Attack; U = Goal Defence; B = Wing Attack; E = Wing Defence.

The major weakness in this method is that no allowance is made for what is actually happening. It may well be that Wing Attack is not being marked by the opposing Wing Defence (who may have dropped back to zone the circle) and that therefore she is in a favourable position to take every subsequent centre pass. Or, on the other hand, it may be that Goal Attack is marked by two players: her opponent Goal Defence and the opposing Centre.

The system demands that Centre is committed to her 'word', and other players are bound, and usually inhibited, by the pre-arranged plan, for they are reluctant to take initiative in case they confuse by playing the ball out of turn. There is the strong possibility of players forgetting the actual letter within the word sequence; this leads to doubt and confusion.

A method frequently used is that of so-called deception. The team attempts to deceive the opposition by having their Centre deliberately face the opposite direction to which she will ultimately pass the ball—face Wing Defence, for example, when the pass is intended for Wing Attack. On the whistle she usually pivots to face the direction of play.

This method seems unnecessarily time-consuming and frequently breaks down. In point of fact, if analysed carefully the practice would appear to favour the defending team to the detriment of the attacks for the following reasons:

1. Centre's vision is impaired—by her own choice she elects not to look at the player who is to receive the pass. This seems incongruous when moments of 'being free' are frequently only fleeting ones. The chance that a dodge will be missed or a pass made too late as a result of the Centre's positioning seems likely.
2. Centre has to make an unnecessary pivot, which may leave her slightly off-balance before making her first pass.
3. Finally, delay at the centre pass is in effect giving time to the opposition. They can use this time to react to the initial dodges of the attacks and to form their own units for defence.

The sum total of this 'deceptive' method seems to be the unnecessary introduction of variables leaving greater opportunity for error.

These practices, although workable, do seem to put excess stress on Centre, are expensive on time, leave a great deal to chance and completely ignore what is actually happening in the game.

CENTRE PASS: ATTACKING

Given that the object of attacking play has something to do with the scoring of goals, and that a centre pass ought to be a move in the right direction, certain facts should be aired, which, in my view, influence the way in which tactics concerning the centre pass and subsequent passes are structured. The order is of no consequence, but each will be considered, and applied as the chapter progresses.

1. The shorter the period that the ball is in the air, the less time there is available for error or interception; therefore direct passes over short distances lend themselves naturally to greater efficiency.
2. The player in possession of the ball (in the event of a centre pass this will be Centre) needs absolute clarity of vision to be able to assess the situation and to be able to pass accurately after a decision has been made. For this she should be looking directly at the player to whom the pass will be made,

for as long as is practicable. This will involve looking at her before and after the whistle.
3. Despite any adjustments or adaptations made by Centre, all other members of her team should have some degree of knowledge as to the probable course of action. They should therefore be involved in some small way with every situation.
4. The centre pass is merely a means to an end, to scoring a goal, therefore each pass should be considered in conjunction with circle feeding and subsequent shooting opportunities. It should not be considered in isolation, and it should be noted that the best position for feeding the circle is the centre front—as near to the circle edge as possible. This naturally minimizes the time the ball is in the air, while offering the maximum area for the feeding players. At the same time it allows maximum space for the shooters to free themselves. (Figs. 18–20)

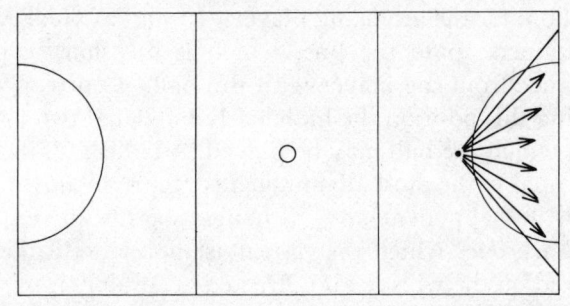

Fig. 18 Minimal passing distance; maximum space available for dodging

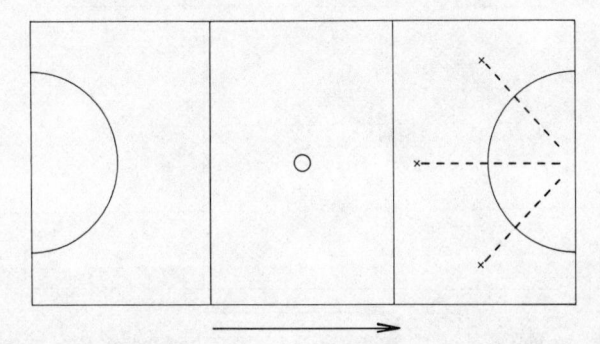

Fig. 19 Distance from the circle edge increases the time that the ball is in the air

44 Attacking Tactics

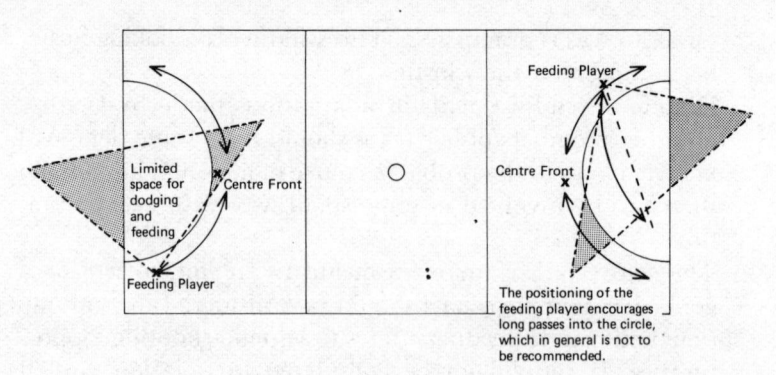

Fig. 20 Distance from the centre front of the circle decreases both the angle for feeding and the space for dodging. It also encourages unnecessarily long passes into the circle. Shaded area shows wasted space

5. The opportunity given by the centre pass should be used to advantage; the fact that players are prohibited from the centre court prior to the whistle being blown ensures certain freedom for the attacking players. In Fig. 21 Goal Attack is positioned up to the line, which is the shortest possible distance from the player with the ball—Centre. By establishing this position she has clearly indicated two free areas into which the ball may be played, A and B. Of the two, B is probably the most advantageous as it is the furthest point from her opponent and, although slightly increasing the distance over which the pass must be made, if the ball is played on the whistle and directed accurately it is virtually

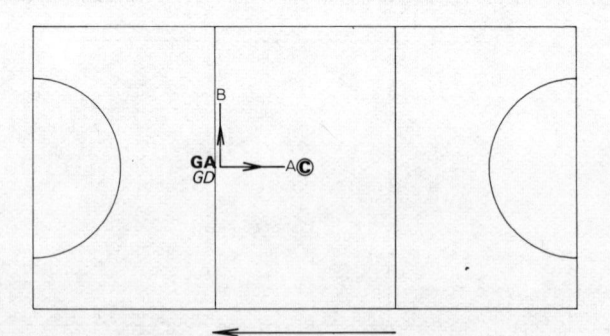

Fig. 21 A and B shows the spaces available when the receiver of the centre pass (Goal Attack) positions herself as shown

undefendable in one-to-one play. Goal Attack travels along the line remaining in the attacking third until the moment of receiving.

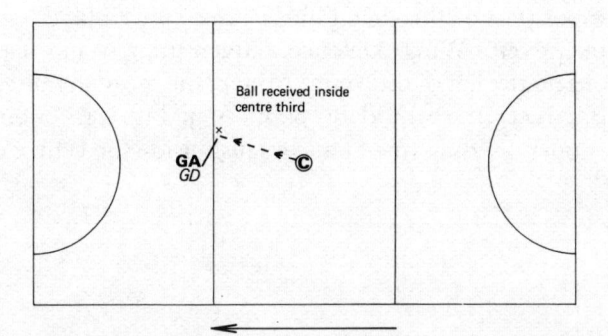

Fig. 22 Goal Attack travels a short distance along the dividing line before receiving a very direct pass inside the centre third

Taking guidance from this, I suggest that tactics from a centre pass be developed along the following lines. The player who is to receive the centre pass positions herself in such a way that she is the shortest possible distance from Centre. (Fig. 23)

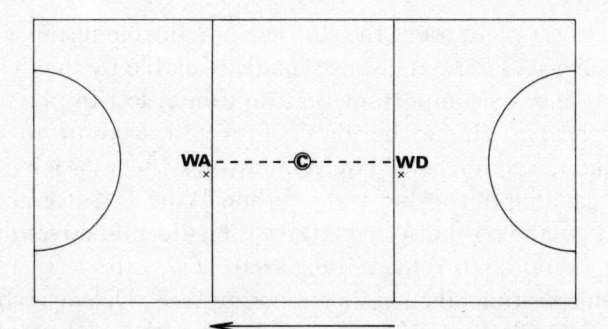

Fig. 23 The player to receive the centre pass positions the shortest possible distance from the Centre

She should be up to and squarely facing the line to allow maximum distance between the possible point of receiving and her opponent. Her body width occupies space which in turn is space taken away from the defending players. A sideways

46 Attacking Tactics

stance allows the defence to position herself nearer to the possible receiving point than is necessary. Centre takes her position in the centre circle and makes the necessary decision as to where the ball will probably be required. This will depend on the position of the defending centre court player—in the example given, Wing Defence. Given that Wing Defence positions on the left of the Wing Attack, the most advantageous point for receiving would be point A in Fig. 24a, along the centre court dividing line. This lies just inside the centre court,

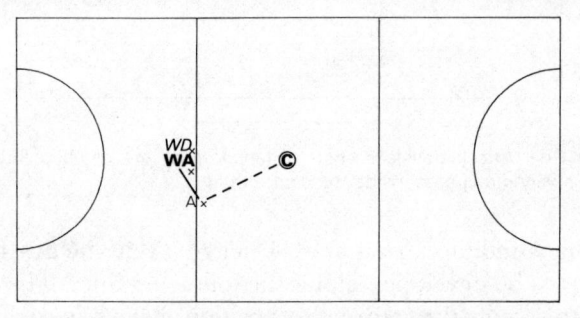

Fig. 24a Ball to be received at point A

the farthest point, over the shortest practicable distance, from the defence. To use the space made available by the defence's positioning, it is important that no time is lost in playing the ball; the pass should be direct, firm and accurate in such a manner that it is received by Wing Attack when she is extended and reaching out to her right. When Wing Defence positions herself on the right of Wing Attack then the most advantageous point would be to Wing Attack's left. (Fig. 24b)

If the position taken by the opposing Wing Defence is behind Wing Attack (not recommended) then the ball should be directed along a straight pathway into the outstretched hands of Wing Attack.

This approach takes advantage of:
1. *Positioning:* the free area created by the attack with her initial positioning.
2. *Short passing:* the pass is made over a relatively short distance so favouring accuracy.

Attacking Tactics   47

3. *Time:* it is economical in its use of time, for the directness of the pass and the confidence with which the ball is played take time from the defenders.

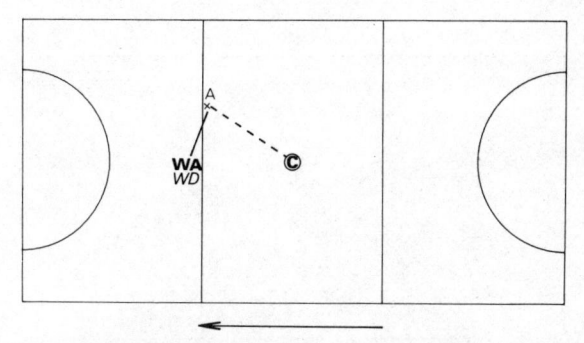

Fig. 24b   Ball to be received at point A

Not only does this method get the ball safely into play, it serves to inform the whole team of exactly what is happening. In facing the attacking court, Centre clearly indicated to the defending trio of Goal Defence, Goal Keeper and Wing Defence, that they are not actively required in the centre pass. This prior warning enables them to keep the centre court clear to those more positively involved, and to prepare positionally for possible emergency.

It is not an uncommon sight to see defending players charging into the centre court the instant that the whistle releases them. Their intentions are good and while they may offer themselves as an 'alternative' for Centre it must be remembered that in so doing they may:
  a. take space—which may lead to congestion;
  b. confuse the Centre—by offering too many alternatives;
  c. carry their opponents up court—so congest;
  d. impinge on territory—take another's playing role;
  e. neglect their main job—that of defending.

There will be many occasions known by the whole team when one of the defending players is required to be part of localized attack at the centre pass, but this is organized and prepared for —not accidental.

So far suggestions made have pre-supposed one-to-one

Attacking Tactics

marking and, as yet, alternatives in case of emergency have not been offered. This, for me, is a vital aspect of all tactical planning. For every pass made there must always be at least one alternative.

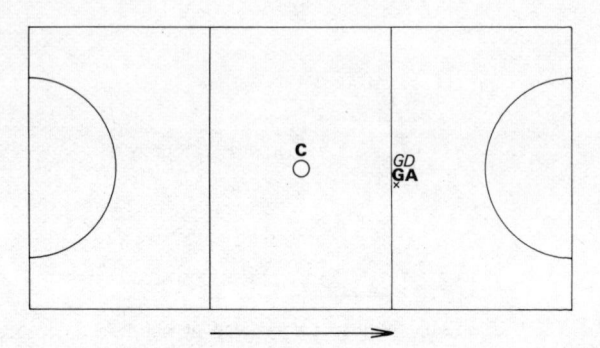

Fig. 25 Goal Attack positioned ready to take the centre pass

Let's assume that the instance is still one-to-one marking with Goal Attack positioned ready to take the centre pass. (Fig. 25) Given that the suggestions concerning the movements of defending players at a centre pass are acceptable, it seems logical that in the example above the alternative for the centre pass should be Wing Attack. It is proposed that she assumes a position as indicated. (Fig. 26) By positioning herself thus she is in a favourable position to see exactly what is happening and can therefore prepare for any eventuality. Centre is able to see

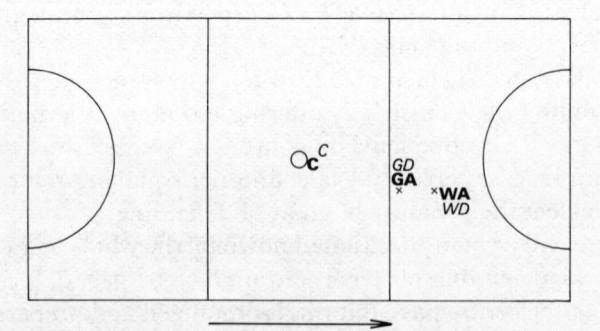

Fig. 26 Wing Attack positioned in readiness to take the centre pass if Goal Attack fails to do so

Attacking Tactics 49

her, and although all three are independent beings, making independent assessments and decisions, they are actually reacting as one.

In the example given, Wing Attack has provided herself with maximum dodging room because she has remained spatially uncommitted and taken neither the left nor the right; the centre court is clear for her to move into and not congested by defending players. Centre does not have to look away from the particular area of play, and every player in the team knows what is happening.

Assuming that for some reason Goal Attack is not free to receive the centre pass, then any of the following alternatives may be readily employed:

1. Wing Attack travels to receive the pass; Goal Shooter links with her, so clearing the centre zone for Centre, who takes the ball on the circle edge and feeds the incoming Goal Attack—who shoots and scores! (Fig. 27)

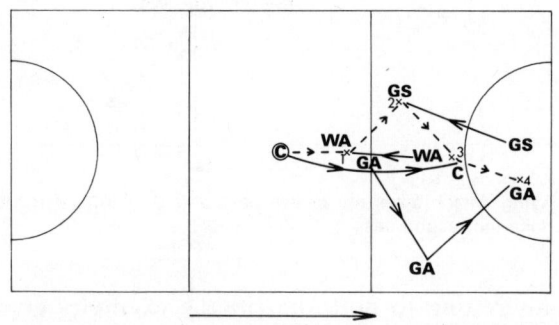

Fig. 27 Wing Attack substitutes for Goal Attack and takes the centre pass

2. Wing Attack receives the pass and returns it to Centre; Goal Attack recovers and takes the ball from Centre as near to the circle as possible. Goal Shooter receives the ball in the circle and shoots. (Fig. 28)
3. Wing Attack receives the pass and Goal Attack recovers to take the second pass. Goal Shooter links, while Centre frees herself on the front of the circle to take the ball. Goal Shooter receives the return ball from Centre as she runs into the circle. (Fig. 29)

50   Attacking Tactics

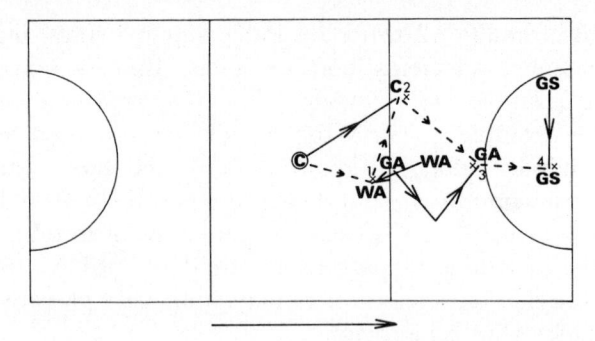

Fig. 28 Wing Attack takes the centre pass and plays the return ball to the Centre

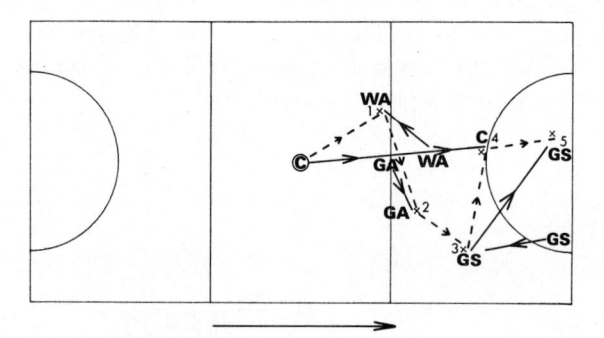

Fig. 29 Wing Attack takes the centre pass and Goal Attack recovers positionally to take the second pass

It is interesting to note that in the examples given there occurs an interchange of personnel and with this a natural interchange of playing areas and roles, yet despite this activity all territories are adequately provided for.

Although simple in concept, this method of play demands that individuals work as a unit. They cannot make decisions in isolation, for ideally every decision made will trigger off a series of reactions. It can be done, and very effectively: the criteria for success is that players look and think; they do not simply run. (An interesting exercise for coaches is to watch a team for a short period and see how many players actually look further than the ball.)

Attacking Tactics 51

It must be emphasized at this point that it is far simpler to react and adjust when at a distance from the ball than it is close to it; and it is therefore suggested that the main initiative comes from those in the thick of it and the adjustments from players deeper in the court. (Fig. 30)

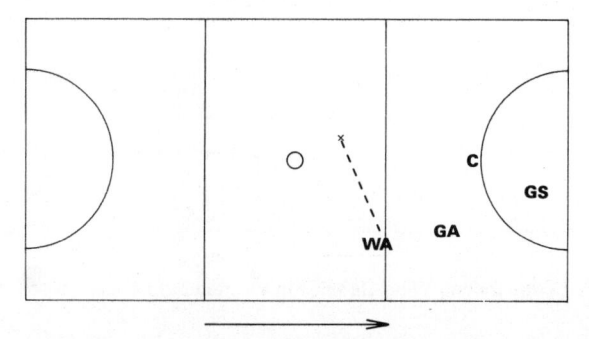

Fig. 30 Goal Shooter, being at a greater distance from the ball than Centre and Goal Attack, should be watching carefully and adjusting accordingly

Here, Goal Shooter should try to assess the intentions of Goal Attack and Centre before acting and should be continually adapting to their manoeuvres. Centre watches Goal Attack and Wing Attack, Goal Attack watches Wing Attack and Centre, while Wing Attack concentrates on catching the ball and making a safe pass.

Spatially, players should be concerned before and after they play the ball. It is so often the inane running following a pass that leaves players in wrong positions and lacking intention and aim!

THE DEFENDING TEAM

It would be unwise to conclude a chapter on centre passes without considering the possible tactics of the defending team.

To date it has been assumed that defending has been based on one-to-one marking. It is to be expected, however, that with skilled players alternative counters will be offered and such contingencies should be anticipated.

Attacking Tactics

One tactic currently popular is that of the opposing Centre joining her Wing Defence or Goal Defence in an attempt to double block a particular player. (Fig. 31)

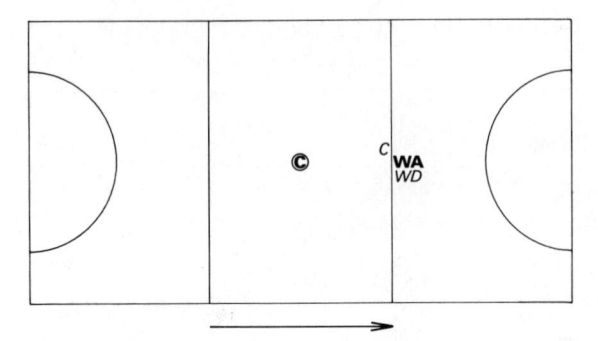

Fig. 31 Centre joining Wing Defence in an attempt to double-block the Wing Attack

This type of initiative may be counteracted in one of several ways, and a variety of response may well confound the defending team. Much of what happens should depend on the intention and quality of the defences. For simplicity of explanation, a practical situation is given to illustrate the possibilities open to the attacks.

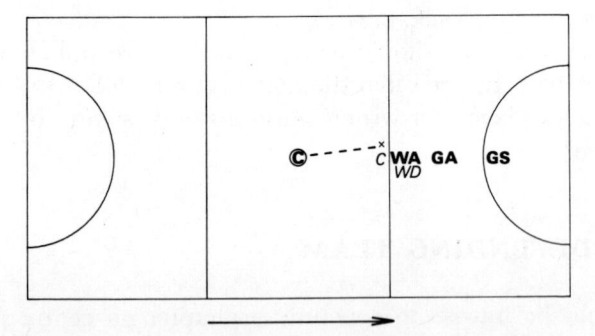

Fig. 32 Centre facing Wing Attack. Method favours attacks

Centre Facing Wing Attack

It should make little if any difference. The opposing Centre

Attacking Tactics 53

cannot see the ball, has no indication when or from which direction it is coming, can serve to block the path of her own Wing Defence.

Centre can afford to loop the ball over the head of the opposing Centre and slightly to the right. Wing Defence cannot move and Centre cannot see. This method favours attack.

Centre Facing Centre

Here the attacking team has to anticipate the intention of the opposing Centre. Whether she intends marking, or whether she is merely standing to distract or confuse. (Fig. 33)

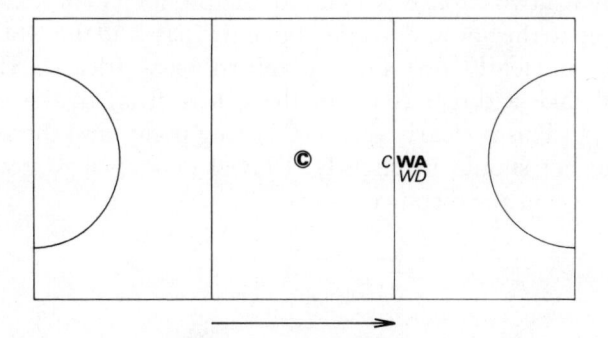

Fig. 33 Centre facing Centre

Given that the opposing Centre is intending to defend, then adjustments need to be made before the whistle for the centre pass. It is assumed that the opposing Centre has taken her position in such a way that she is able to see her opponent with the ball and is favourably placed to see and defend the Wing Attack. On recognizing this the initiative lies primarily with Wing Attack who must attempt to commit and confuse both the opposing Wing Defence and Centre. She may choose to travel along the dividing centre court line to a point as far away from probable play as possible. (Fig. 34)

If both the opposing Wing Defence and Centre are concerned with defending they will both travel with her. This in

54   Attacking Tactics

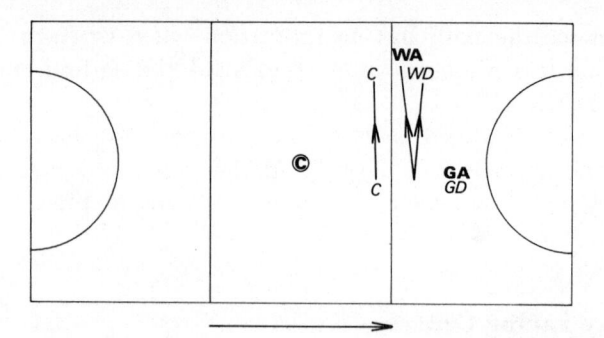

Fig. 34 Wing Attack drawing Wing Defence and Centre away from probable area of play. One player occupying two

itself gives advantage to the attacking team for one player is occupying two. Space is made available for Goal Attack to move up to the line and to take the centre pass and the attacking Centre is clearly free for the return pass. Ideally, Centre should take a direct route to the centre front of the circle. (Fig. 35) This is clearly the best feeding point, and the return pass to her should be slightly delayed or looped to give her time to cover the distance.

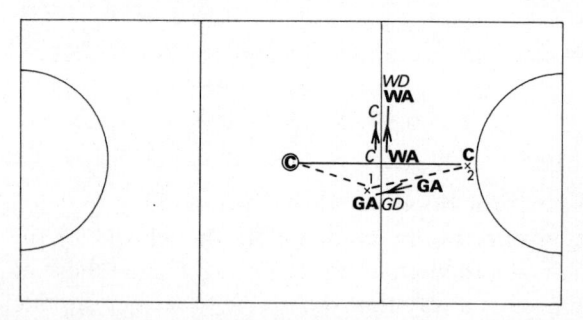

Fig. 35 Goal Attack takes an easy pass and delays her return ball until Centre is on the circle edge—the best feeding position for the circle

Drawing the Defending Centre

In the following examples suggestions are made as to how to counteract the eventuality of the defending Centre player resisting the temptation to be drawn by the Wing Attack.

Attacking Tactics 55

It may well be that as the Wing Attack moves away from the centre of the court the opposing Centre stays her ground. (Fig. 36)

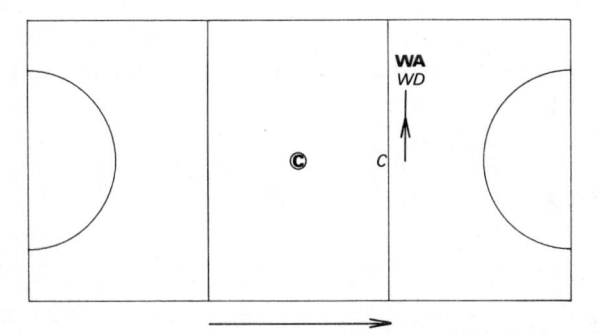

Fig. 36 Opposing Centre stays as Wing Attack moves, so resisting the temptation to be drawn

Should this situation arise, then between them Wing Attack and Goal Attack must work either to commit the opposing Centre or make space available for the pass to be played. This can be done by dropping back slightly into court and cutting forward again towards the opposing Centre. She will probably anticipate Wing Attack going for the pass and commit herself to mark—at which point Goal Attack, still marked one-to-one, moves nearer to the centre court and travels out to take the pass. (The practical function of Wing Attack in this case is as a decoy.) As this move may lead to Wing Attack being slightly

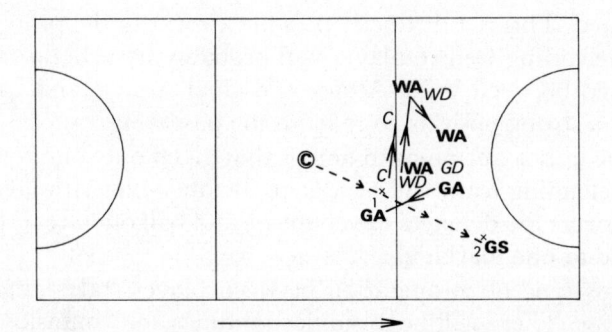

Fig. 37 Wing Attack deliberately attempting to commit both Wing Defence and Centre: Goal Attack takes centre pass and Goal Shooter links with her

56 Attacking Tactics

out of position for a second pass, and space is limited for Centre to travel forward, Goal Shooter could well be the link player. (Fig. 37)

An alternative may be for Wing Attack to drop deeper into court carrying the opposing Wing Defence with her, and Goal Attack to take the centre pass on the same side of the court as Wing Attack using a sprint-dodge in a forward direction. Wing Attack is then in a good position to take a second pass, and the space is available for Centre to travel along a direct route for goal. (Fig. 38)

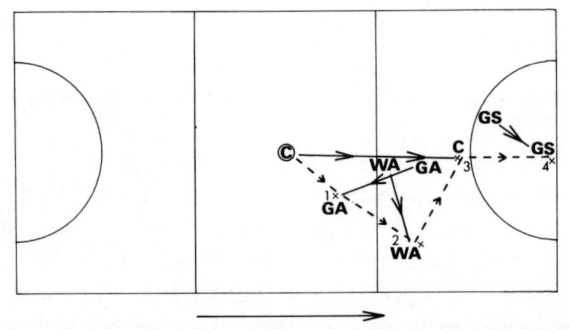

Fig. 38 Goal Attack takes the centre pass on the same side as Wing Attack, who is in a good position to receive the second pass; space is available for the Centre to link with her before feeding the circle

A further possibility is that Wing Attack, having attempted to draw the opposing Centre, pulls back close to her original position fractionally before the whistle, and takes the pass as planned. This is a distinctly possible answer to the problem as the defending Centre player will probably have her attention divided between Wing Attack and Goal Attack, and will not be in a strong position to react to the pass. (Fig. 39)

The important point to note is that given only one response the defending team will be able to dictate—but with a variety of answers the defences are confused and will often revert back to one-to-one marking.

This type of co-operation between players takes time and practice. There will be misunderstandings and confusions, but with patience and care and, most of all, individual observation of the situation a pattern will emerge where players freely interchange and play with a degree of certainty which breeds confidence and success.

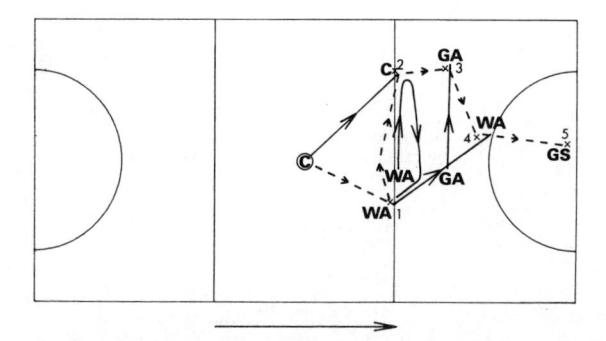

Fig. 39 Wing Attack takes the centre pass as planned having attempted to confuse the opposing Centre before the whistle for the start of play

CENTRE PASS: DEFENDING PLAYERS

Centre passes made to either of the two defending players (Wing Defence or Goal Defence) can follow a similar pattern to those of the forward attacking players:
1. Centre faces the defending half of the court.
2. The player to receive the pass positions close to the centre court dividing line, as near Centre as possible. This gives maximum opportunity for dodging.
3. The reserve player positions slightly behind the one receiving the centre pass. (Figs. 40a, 40b)

Wing Attack and Goal Attack know that they are not involved in the pass and position and adjust in accordance with the activities at the other end.

It is highly improbable, and not to be recommended, that the opposing Centre attempts to double-block Goal Defence. It can be assumed therefore that the marking is one-to-one and the pass should be relatively straightforward.

A short direct ball may be simply executed or, if so desired, time may be allowed for Goal Defence or Wing Defence to sprint up court. This distance need not necessarily increase the distance of pass, but the delay will undoubtedly give time to the opposition!

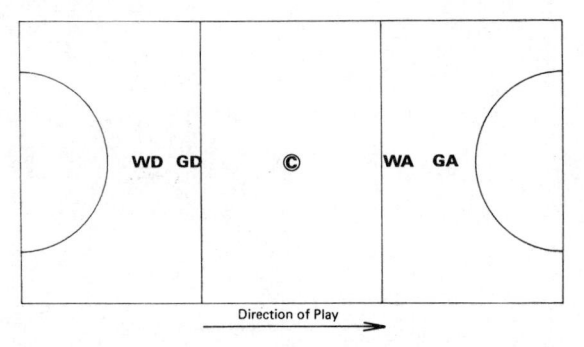

Fig. 40a Centre pass to be played to a defending player — probably Goal Defence. The reserve is Wing Defence

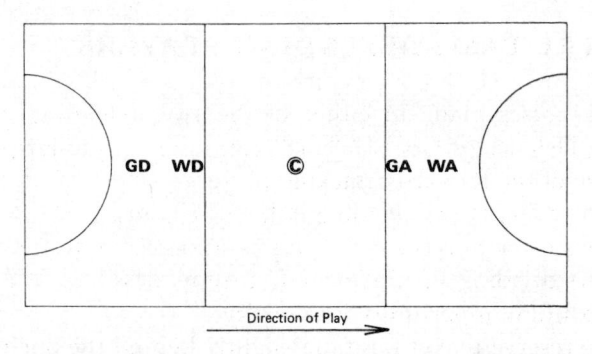

Fig. 40b Centre pass to be played by Wing Defence. Goal Defence is the reserve player

It may be argued that to play the ball into the defending half of the court is uneconomical in terms of time and space. So it may be, but this must be evaluated against the following:
1. A player receiving a ball while travelling towards her own goal need never loose sight of the circle area. She does not have to change direction on catching, and as a result is often better informed and balanced to make a very quick second pass.

Attacking Tactics 59

2. As a game progresses attacking players may lose their edge and benefit by a short break from centre pass work.
3. If a plan of campaign is implemented (as discussed in Chapter 4 on unit divisions), unless there is a breakdown in skill, it should be possible to secure the safe passage of the ball to the shooters in the circle.

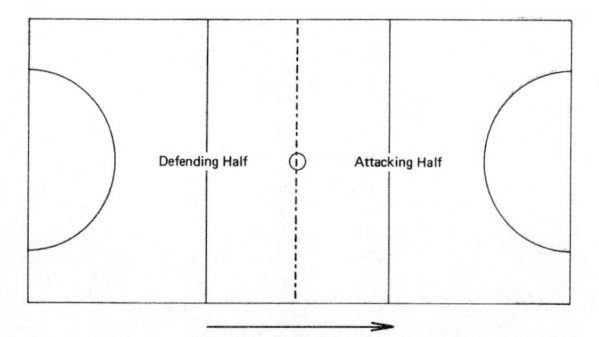

Fig. 41 Pass to be received in the defending half of the court, so the responsibility after the centre pass remains with the defending trio and Centre

Given that Wing Defence takes a centre pass, and receives the ball while still in the defending half of the court (Fig. 41), the responsibility for play remains with the defending trio and Centre; in the example given, the territory of play is that of Centre, so it might therefore follow that she takes a return pass —it may not be wise to have both Goal Defence and Wing Defence up court. (Fig. 42)

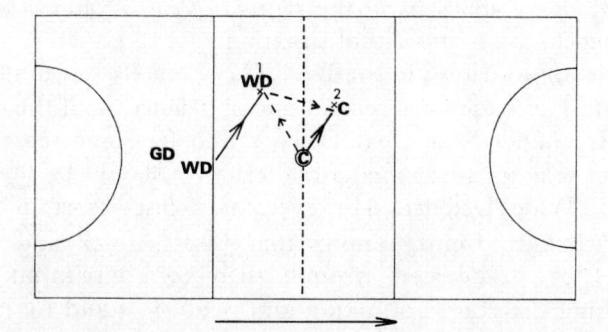

Fig. 42 The second pass is played very speedily back to the Centre

60 Attacking Tactics

The second or return pass from Wing Defence to Centre can be made very smoothly for both players know what is going to happen, though not necessarily where it will occur. This must depend on the positioning of the opposing Centre and Wing Attack. Fig. 43a offers some suggestions as to where the return ball may be played and received.

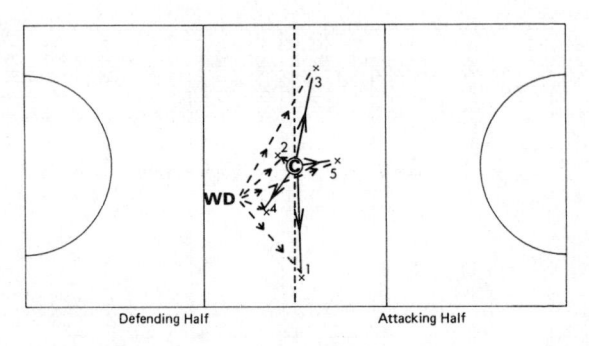

Fig. 43a Some suggestions as to where the second pass from Wing Defence to Centre may be received

The fact that every team member knows what is happening generally and has some idea when she will be needed gives those involved a confidence which can only improve their game. It is important to note that as with the centre passes made to the attacking players (Wing Attack, Goal Attack) a similar pattern of security emerges where the reserve or alternative player positions herself a few feet behind ready for emergency. Again, from this position she has maximized her own dodging space, is in the sights of Centre, and is ideally situated to assess the actual situation.

A final word on alternatives. The methods recommended naturally provide for a second line of defence: so if the centre pass is intended for Goal Defence and for some reason she cannot take it, the immediate alternative should be the 'prepared' Wing Defence. However, as a last resort, if Wing Defence fails, Centre knows that Goal Attack and Wing Attack are somewhere around their own territorial areas watching the course of action and ready to stand by in real emergency.

SUMMARY AND CONCLUSION

When the centre pass is to the attacking players, Wing Attack or Goal Attack, each serves as an alternative to the other, and the emergency player is either of the defences. Similarly, when the centre pass is for the defending players the roles are reversed; the emergency player is Wing Attack or Goal Attack while the immediate alternative is the defending player standing by as an option.

It is worth repeating that centre passes should always be considered in conjunction with circle feeding and subsequent shooting opportunities, so it is necessary to suggest possible developments after the centre pass.

For simplicity, the possibilities suggested in Fig. 43a will again be used.

In Fig. 43b Centre receives the return ball in the attacking half of the court. Working again on the unit system all players should recognize that responsibility at this moment is transferred from the defences to the attacks. Having accomplished their job (small though their contribution may be), the defending players should attempt to keep the playing area clear for the attacks. In this way Goal Attack, Wing Attack, Centre and Goal Shooter become the responsible players.

The method adopted will vary according to the situation, and the suggestions offered are merely possibilities.

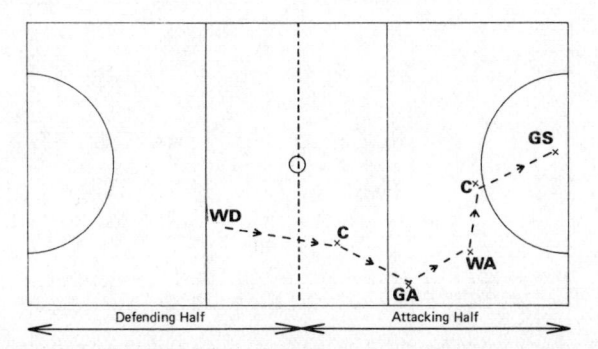

Fig. 43b The ball is received by the Centre in the attacking half of the court; she works with the attacks to secure safe passage into the shooting circle

62 Attacking Tactics

In Fig. 43c Centre has received the return pass while still in the defending half of the court. Responsibility will therefore remain with the defending players and it would seem appropriate that Goal Defence—the player not directly involved with the first pass—should receive the ball from Centre.

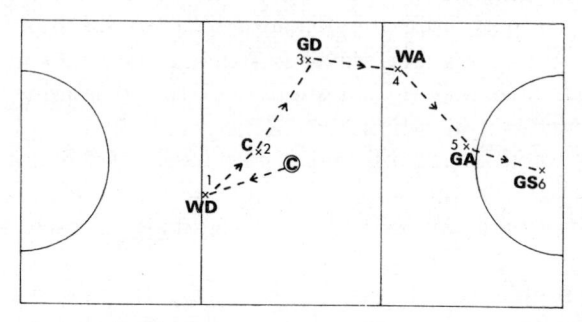

Fig. 43c Centre takes the return ball while still in the defending half of the court

In so doing, Goal Defence in fact takes on the role of Centre; this applies technically and spatially, and she should, as Centre, anticipate feeding Wing Attack—or the assumed Wing Attack as the case may be. Similarly Wing Defence should assume the role of Goal Defence, and Centre would function momentarily as Wing Defence. (Fig. 44a)

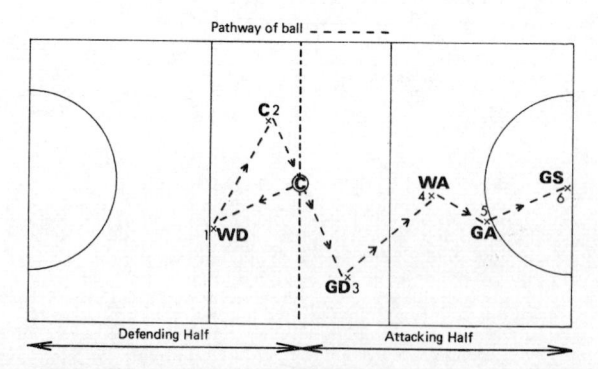

Fig. 44a Assumed roles after a centre pass: Wing Defence has dropped back to become Goal Defence; Centre is momentarily acting as Wing Defence while Goal Defence functions as Centre

In Fig. 44b the return ball is received in the attacking half of court—the subsequent responsibility lying with the attacks.

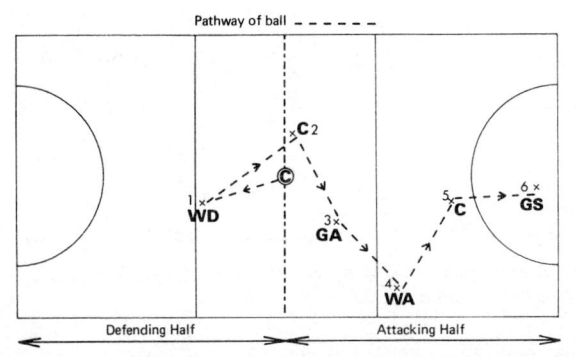

Fig. 44b The return pass is received in the attacking half of the court

Fig. 44c shows how the return ball is again received in the defending half; responsibility remains with the defending players. All players are aware of the situation, and can make the necessary adjustments.

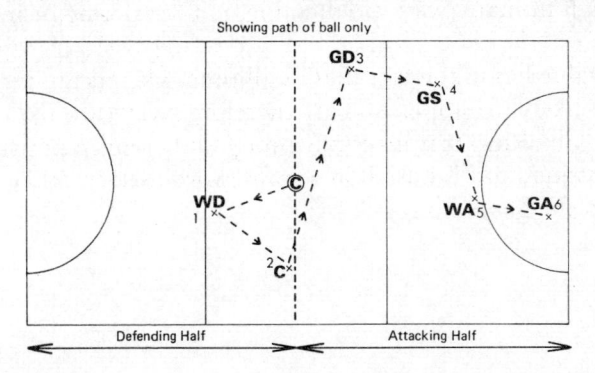

Fig. 44c The return ball is received in the defending half: responsibility lies with the defences

In Fig. 44d the return ball is received in the attacking half and immediately the defending players withdraw. The attacks take the initiative.

In the examples used, the ball has been passed from the centre court into the hands of a shooter in the circle.

64 Attacking Tactics

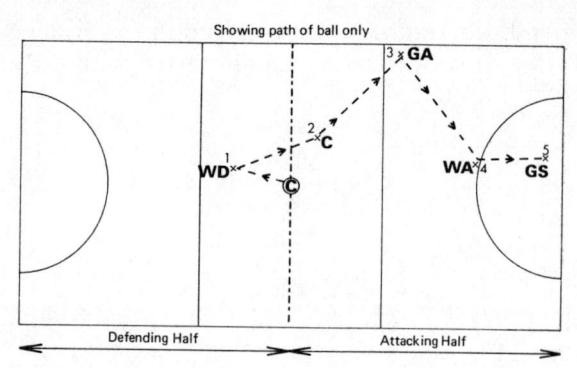

Fig. 44d Responsibility lies with the attacks as the second pass was taken in the attacking half of the court

Importance has been attached to providing space in which players may move freely; to the natural interchanging of individuals when the game calls for it; and particularly to the structuring of a system which enables every player to read, understand, and adapt to the actual happenings in the game.

What has been presented is a pattern of play which may be used in all centre passes, itself simple and clear in structure and, although in many ways predictable, not restricting or inhibiting.

Its value lies in the fact that at all times players are aware of what is likely to happen and are therefore given time to prepare for eventualities. It utilizes advantages inherent in positioning and passing, and is based on a framework used in other situations in the game.

Chapter 6
Defending Tactics

It has been suggested in previous chapters that in all circumstances advantage is with the side who have possession of the ball—the Attackers. Whilst this is true, it is none the less my belief that defending players can and do influence the patterns of play and at times even appear to dictate procedure. Skilful defensive play often results in attacking breakdowns. Hesitations, indecisive moves or hasty decisions are usually the sequel to intensive defending tactics. If, by their versatility and quick-wittedness, defending players can be responsible for sowing seeds of doubt in the offensive teams then mistakes will be made; for which the price may well be loss of possession.

Tactically there are ways that defences can outwit opponents, but 'thoughtful defending' has been, and in many instances still is, a neglected aspect of the game.

Until relatively recently the only recognized method was individual man-to-man marking, and this approach is highly commendable and very effective. However, variety presents its own problems and a constantly changing response will undoubtedly worry an attacking team. They have to be aware of what is happening, and this demand on them can sometimes lead to rhythmical breakdowns in their own play. When a response becomes predictable then measures of counteraction can be practised and readily implemented.

It seems fitting at this point to mention the rules relating to body checking or blocking. This method of defending has been interpreted and practised in so many different ways by so many different people that understandably there have been many differences of opinion.

I would like to make it clear that while I do not favour the rather negative, often dangerous, practice of harassing players so as to restrict movements, regardless of the ball or of what is actually happening in the game, I acknowledge that in some cases the practices arising from the interpretations have served to at least jolt players into thinking their way out of unfamiliar situations. In early days the problems seemed confined to the shooting circles but when blocking permeated the whole court, counteraction became a real problem and everybody had to try to adapt: the game took on the appearance of a 'penguin war-dance' with couples cavorting cheek to cheek, back to front, front to front, with little, if any, awareness of the ball, or the court; performance quite foreign to the game of netball as it was previously known.

The rules stand, however, and only positive coaching will prevent the game permanently changing its image and, so far as I am concerned, losing its character.

Having discussed in some detail in Chapter 3 the specific defending roles of individual players, it may well be of value to comment generally on the objectives of the 'whole team unit' when defending.

There are two aims: to regain possession of the ball, and to prevent the opponents shooting at goal.

Where regaining possession is the defending team's prime concern, and this is the case for 99 per cent of the game, then undoubtedly there is the need for the industrious application of basic defending skills. Players must be prepared not merely to shadow, but completely over-shadow, their opponents. Ideally there should be a barely measurable distance in any direction between a defender and her opponent, for given this closeness in defending it is unlikely that an accurate pass can be made.

It is appreciated that nothing is more taxing or energy-sapping than really intensive man-to-man marking, but such close defending does bring its rewards: errors are forced; and this method is recognized as being the most productive in terms of forcing mistakes.

There is no substitute for good basic defending skills. The ability to read and adapt to movement cues, to change direction quickly and to catch balls never intended for one, are just a few of the skill requirements of a defender, and individuals must be prepared to equip themselves mentally and physically for such demands.

As this book is concerned with tactics and not skills, let me just remind readers of the great importance I attach to personal skills; for, in defending, one weak link will negate the efforts of others and will usually result in a complete breakdown.

REGAINING POSSESSION

This is by far the most important objective of defending play. It will be shown later that there are occasions when the concern may be to delay the opposition or to prevent them from attempting to shoot at goal, but these situations are few when compared with the foremost objective of regaining possession.

Assuming possession is lost during play (not a dead ball, as in a centre pass or throw-up), then the responsibility for recovery should be shared by every member of the defending team. This applies to the Goal Shooter as much as to the Goal Keeper, for when in defensive role every player is expected to contribute.

It may well be that close man-to-man marking is required, for one of the aims should be to minimize opportunities for the attackers. Often the rewards for really close defending are errors by the attackers in the form of either panic and carelessness, or holding the ball for longer than three seconds. As this particular aspect falls under the heading of 'skills' it will not be dealt with in detail.

Methods of recovery will vary according to the team concerned, the opposition, the score, and the actual situation in the game. Tactically this may involve:
    a. apparently loose defending—giving false security;
    b. pressurizing players;
    c. part court zoning.

Apparently Loose Defending

When a team has a member known to have very good anticipation and also speed of movement, then occasionally it can be a worthwhile tactic for that player to scheme for an interception; this may be from her own opponent or somebody else's.

The state of the game and where play is centred should determine whether any of the other defending players mark in man-to-man fashion or whether they encourage the opponents into a false sense of security, hoping for the careless pass which is what the poised anticipator counts on (Mary French, who for many years was England Coach, Selector and Captain, was reputedly brilliant at just this). Fig. 45 shows the interception made by blue Wing Attack—the ball being taken from the opposing Wing Attack. It is not to be recommended that this tactic be practised too frequently in the close proximity of the attacking circle unless a team has a particularly talented player, as a mistake would give an easy shot at goal.

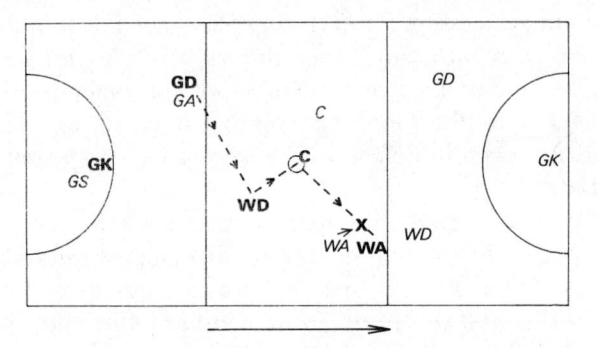

Fig. 45 Wing Attack playing for an interception: X marks the point of interception

Two Against One—Pressurizing

This is a tactic often included for one of two reasons:
1. When a particular player, or even more than one player, is making too great a contribution, and her influence needs to be minimized, or if possible eliminated.
2. As a shock tactic to cause a careless or confused response. This in its turn takes much of the initiative from the attackers who have to react in some way.

Defending Tactics 69

Fig. 46 shows how the defending players can really pressurize a whole section of the playing area, and if they are prepared to react quickly they can often be successful with this tactic.

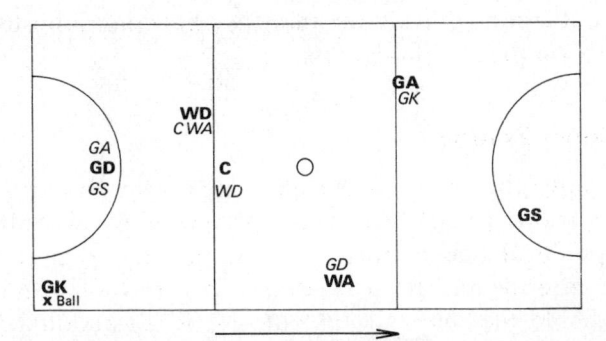

Fig. 46 Pressurizing the defending court; the ball is with the Goal Keeper

Fig. 46 shows how both the white Goal Defence and Wing Defence are marked by two opponents; Goal Shooter at the other end is left completely unmarked, while Goal Attack and Wing Attack are marked by 'strangers'.

In brief, all that has happened is that the players in the immediate danger area—in this case the defending third—have been pressurized; those in the next danger area have been marked one-to-one and the area which cannot be used because of the throwing distance rule has been slightly under-manned —this, however, only temporarily.

Should the attacking team manage to get the ball down court then the defenders will naturally have to adjust to ensure that there are players available to carry out specific defending roles. In this example it might be interesting to consider the roles adopted by the defending players. There are:

2 Goal Attacks
2 Wing Attacks
1 Centre
1 Wing Defence
1 Goal Defence

Only Goal Shooter and Wing Attack are actually employed in their own specific positions.

Defending Tactics

Every player must be ready to react should the interception occur, and occasionally it becomes necessary to 'mark time' with the ball, while a team positionally reorganizes itself after the interception. This reorganization is a most important factor, for so often teams win the ball as a result of shock tactics and lose it just as quickly because they have not adjusted to capitalize on their initial success.

Part Court Zoning

As with any other zone a part court zone is where a particular territory is pressurized by as many players as are available.

For practical reasons this is usually the centre court area because most people are permitted in that territory, and because, should the zone fail, the outcome is not automatically disastrous; there may still be time to stop opponents getting the ball into the shooting circle.

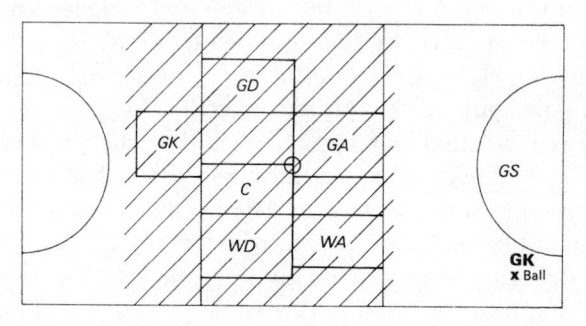

Fig. 47a Part court zone — in depth

In Fig. 47a a zone is made in *depth*. The emphasis is a territorial one and each player is responsible for the area immediately within her surroundings. Players have to be conscious of the ball and of space. Opponents are unimportant.

Fig. 47b shows a zone where the concentration is in *width*. The zone is served by a player in front and one behind. The purpose of the front player, Centre, is to make her opponent's life difficult by following the ball and attempting to intercept the pass; meanwhile, the player behind the zone, Goal

Defending Tactics 71

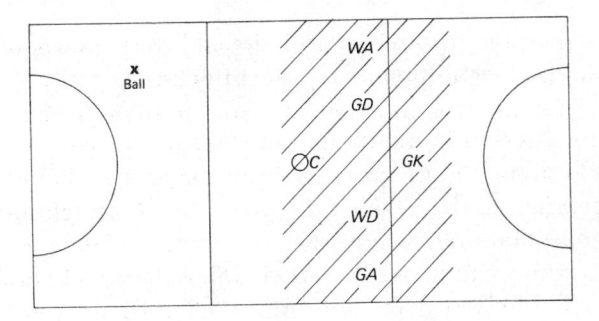

Fig. 47b Part court zone — in width

Keeper, attempts to intercept any pass made over the top of the zone.

Again, the concern of the zone is a spatial one; opposite numbers are unimportant and the emphasis is on the territory and the ball. It is important to note that when an interception is made, time must be made for players to re-position themselves and prepare again for their specialized jobs.

DEAD BALL MOVES

In dead ball moves where the procedure is predictable and only the position unknown, specific tactics dealing with the following need to be exploited:
1. Centre Pass.
2. Throw-in.
3. Penalty Pass.
4. Free Pass
5. Throw-up.
6. Penalty Shot.

Defending at Centre Pass

When defending at a centre pass, it has to be remembered that the aim is to take initiative from the attacks, to try to confuse the opposing organization and if possible cause them to commit hasty or careless actions. How and where the defending players position themselves will depend very much on the positioning of their opponents—the attacks.

If the intention is to defend in man-to-man fashion, then the emphasis will be positional and not territorial, though a spatial awareness of the distance from the centre, should have some bearing on the position adopted. Given straightforward one-to-one marking, where the centre court boundary line restricts movement in one direction, unless the attacks hesitate, pass inaccurately or make some other unforced error, they are virtually undefendable. It is therefore the job of the defending players to confuse the pass whenever possible; to worry both the opposing Centre and the probable recipient by constantly bombarding them with problems—even before the whistle has indicated play.

It is clearly illustrated in Chapter 5 that once a defender commits herself, then the situation for the attack is eased. While a defender's intentions are not known she presents problems, as adaptations by the opposing players have to be made according to the play; and if the play is confused, then anything might happen!

Once again the weapon of the defender is surprise: the more alternatives she can offer in response to the challenge of centre pass tactics the greater will be the pressure on the attacks, and this is when mistakes are made.

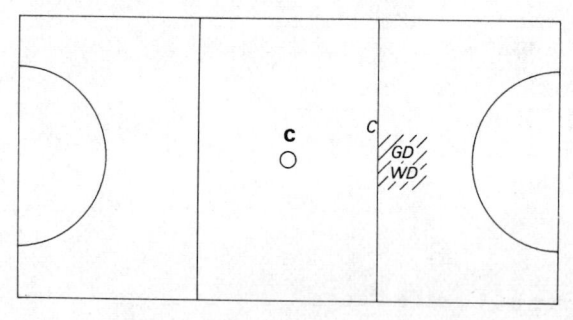

Fig. 48 Goal Defence and Wing Defence filling the space probably needed by the attacks

When considering defending tactics from a centre pass, it is worth bearing in mind the following points:

Defending Tactics

1. The longer the ball is in the air the more time there is available for error.
2. An uncommitted opponent does not help the attack; on the contrary, she leaves her unsure and with divided concentration.
3. Variety of response is unnerving to the opponent.
4. The surprise element is always a weapon.

The following responses have been used with success, and are suggestions which may be used as guide lines for further developments.

1. Fill the space probably wanted by the opposing Wing Attack or Goal Attack—the shortest distance from the centre to the attacking third; this can be done by Goal Defence and Wing Defence together if so desired. (Fig. 48)
2. Keep an ever-changing attitude. Prior to the whistle the defenders are actually changing and interchanging their positions in relation to the attack. (Fig. 49)

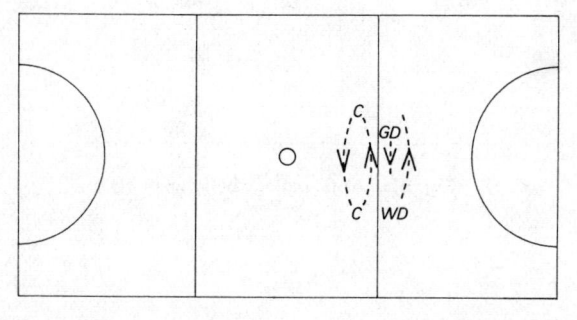

Fig. 49 Defending players constantly on the move, changing relationships and positions

3. Lull attacks into believing that they are free by standing away, anticipating the whistle, and then timing a run so that sprinting speed coincides with the start of play. (Figs. 50, 51) This gives the advantage of a sprint start over a standing start, if timed accurately.
4. Pressurize players who may appear to be making too large a contribution. So, Fig. 52a shows Wing Attack being pressurized, while in Fig. 52b, the pressure is on Goal Attack.

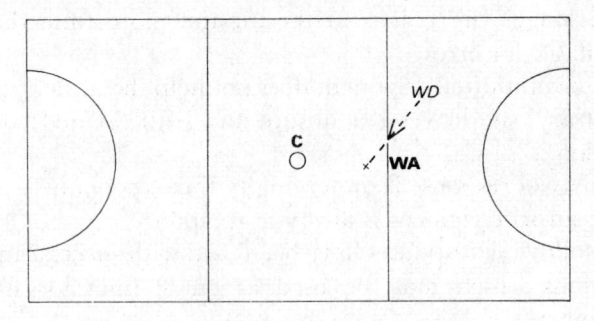

Fig. 50 Anticipating the whistle for a sprint-start

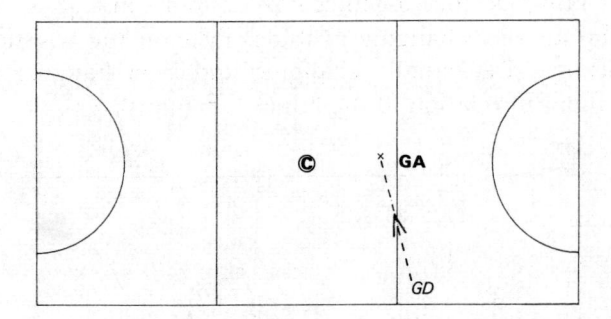

Fig. 51 Anticipating the whistle

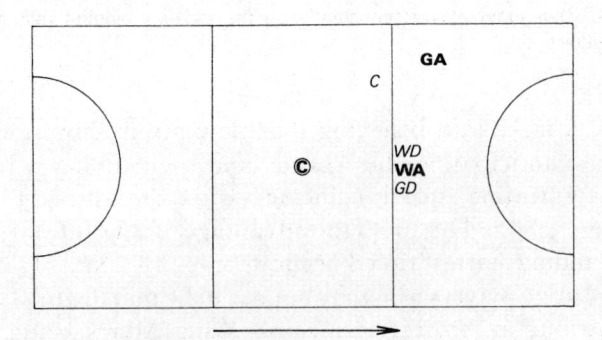

Fig. 52a Pressurizing the Wing Attack

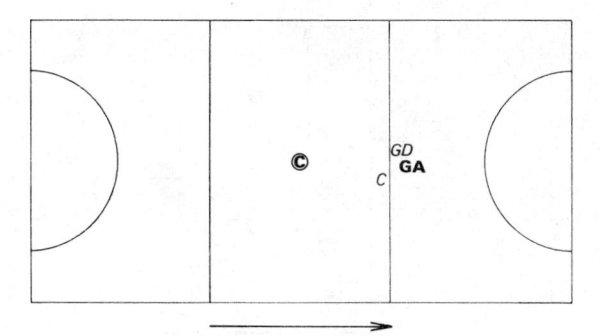

Fig. 52b Pressurizing the Goal Attack

5. Apply a 'circle zone' directly the whistle is blown for start of play.
6. Man-to-man defend for the first pass after which drop back to a circle zone.

Throw-in

It may be appropriate occasionally to pressurize certain areas of play by using a zone defence, as shown in Figs. 53 and 54. Alternatively, it may be necessary to pressurize individual players, as in Figs. 55 and 56.

These measures are not prolonged activities, they are elements of surprise, introduced in an attempt to confuse the opposition. If they are successful, then time must be allowed

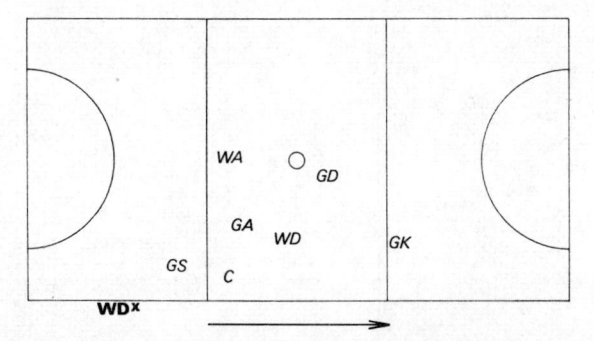

Fig. 53 Throw-in taken by Wing Defence, the defending team zoning part of the court

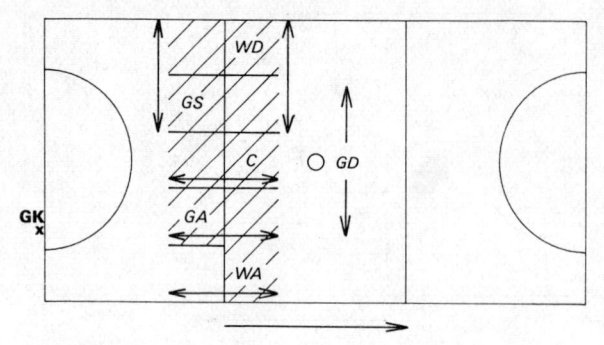

Fig. 54 Throw-in taken by Goal Keeper — part court zone

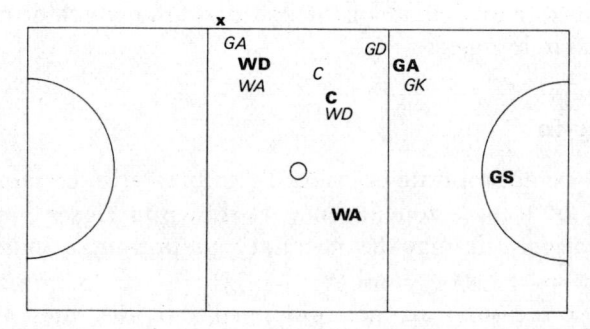

Fig. 55 Throw-in taken by Goal Defence; players being pressurized by defenders two-to-one

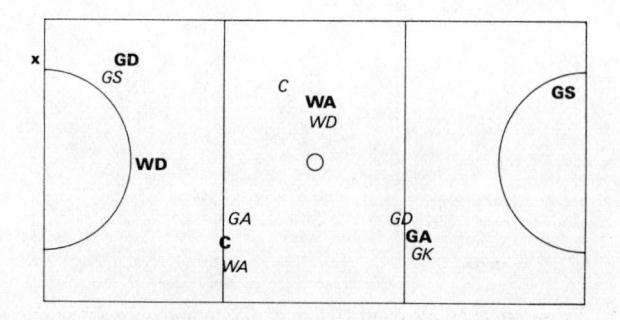

Fig. 56 Throw-in taken by Goal Keeper; players pressurized

for players to re-position themselves in readiness for attacking play, and, on the other hand, if unsuccessful, then quick adjustments have to be made to prepare for more orthodox defending in the circle areas.

It cannot be emphasized enough that when playing any form of zone the concern is spatial. The defender is concerned with her own territory, and the ball. While play is in progress she should be continually adjusting; preparing herself to attempt to take any ball, thrown by any player, which may enter or try to pass through her domain.

When the concern in defending is the opposition, then the space available is unimportant for this is dictated by the attacking players. The concentration must be focused maximally on the player with the prime intention being the preventing of that player receiving the ball.

Penalty Pass—Free Pass

In any situation where play is stopped, and on restarting the ball given to the other side, the defending team may choose to counter-attack in one of three ways: by very close man-to-man marking; by pressurizing one or more players; or by zone defending a territory.

Combining and adopting these methods to meet the demands of the moment, should furnish the defending players with enough material to at least worry the attackers, and once the attentions of the attacking side are diversified then mistakes are likely to occur.

Throw-up

In a throw-up, where possession is battled for, therefore not known at the start of play, it may be that similar contingency tactics are practised to those where possession is lost. This will depend on the situation and is usually influenced by the expectation of winning the throw-up—or losing, as the case may be.

ZONE STRUCTURE

How a zone is structured will probably depend on the time available for formation, the particular situation, and the climate of the play at the time, but the following points might be considered useful guidelines.
1. Fill and cover as much danger space as is possible (this is usually the area around the ball, though not so when the zone is concerned with width and not depth). Keep the zone well spread.
2. Try to establish a zone in either width or depth—don't get caught between the two.
3. The players involved should be concerned with territory and the ball, not with opponents.
4. In the zone formation try to keep the specific defending players (Goal Keeper, Wing Defence, Goal Defence) as near to the goal they are defending as possible, so that if unsuccessful they may quickly get back to their orthodox positions.
5. Generally speaking, use only an orthodox defensive circle zone in the defending third of the court (there is no space for error).
6. Whether the zone is successful or not, remember that dispersal must be quick and players need to reform either in different defensive formations or to initiate attack.

Defending play can be exciting play, and whereas at the outset initiative lies with the team in possession of the ball, it can readily be snatched away, by the application of intelligent tactical strategies.

Let it not be forgotten that the attacking weapon of a defence is surprise. This, accompanied by variety of response, can become a strength which may in its turn take the initiative from the attacking players. Directly a response becomes known and subsequently predictable, it becomes increasingly easy to counteract—the antidote can almost be administered at a subconscious level—and instead of looming as a major obstacle to the attacking force it merely appears as a low hurdle, to be taken in their stride!

PREVENTING OPPONENTS SHOOTING AT GOAL

In preventing opponents shooting at goal the emphasis of the defending team swings to the shooting circle. The concern becomes territorially orientated and opposite numbers become unimportant, for it is only within the confines of the circle that goals may be attempted.

The most concentrated method currently practised is zone defence which involves Centre, Wing Defence, Goal Defence and Goal Keeper. The object is to pressurize the circle in an attempt to prevent the ball entering the shooting area. Possession outside the circle is unimportant, and as a tactic this method often causes the opposition to make careless mistakes because of their apparent freedom; or in their over-anxiety to get the ball to the shooters they do not really adjust to the zone and their passes are intercepted.

In principle this zone is a spatial exercise where the defending players attempt to keep at least one player between the ball and the goal, cover sufficient distance between them so as to cater for any possible pass into the circle widthwise, and defend in depth so as to enable any high ball to be intercepted easily. As the ball moves so does the zone; each player travels in an arc according to the movement of the ball and the complete zone moves as a rigid unit—as one player moves all move.

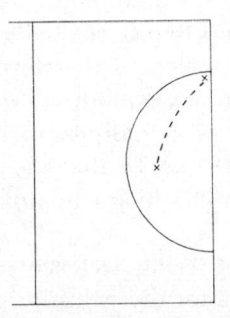

Fig. 57 Semi-circle described by Goal Keeper

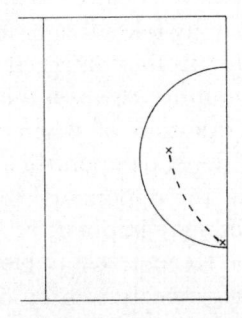

Fig. 58 Semi-circle described by Goal Defence

80 Defending Tactics

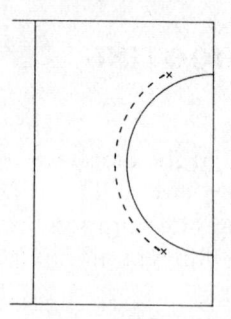

Fig. 59 Semi-circle described by Wing Defence

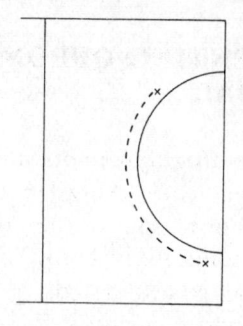

Fig. 60 Semi-circle described by Centre

Centre and Wing Defence describe semi-circles around the outer edge of the shooting circle, while Goal Keeper and Goal Defence describe imaginary ones within the shooting circle. (Figs. 57–60) (Obviously the positions of Goal Defence and Goal Keeper are interchangeable as are those of Wing Defence and Centre.)

There are several occasions when a defending team may wish to introduce a zone defence and the reasons for doing so will differ according to the opposition.

1. If an attacking team is dominant a zone causes them to assess and adapt.
2. It often breaks an attacking team's rhythm to find suddenly that their centre court players are without opponents.
3. To some teams it may be a totally foreign tactic which they have never before encountered and cannot adjust to.
4. It usually takes longer for attackers to pass the ball into the circle (if they succeed at all), which is therefore time-consuming; this is a tactic sometimes exploited.

The question of when the zone is actually implemented usually depends upon the captain. It may be that she decides to act at the opponents' centre pass in which case any of the following may happen:

1. Goal Keeper, Goal Defence and Wing Defence take up their respective positions prior to the whistle. Centre positions herself as close to the defending circle as possible, within the centre third, and Goal Attack and Wing Attack

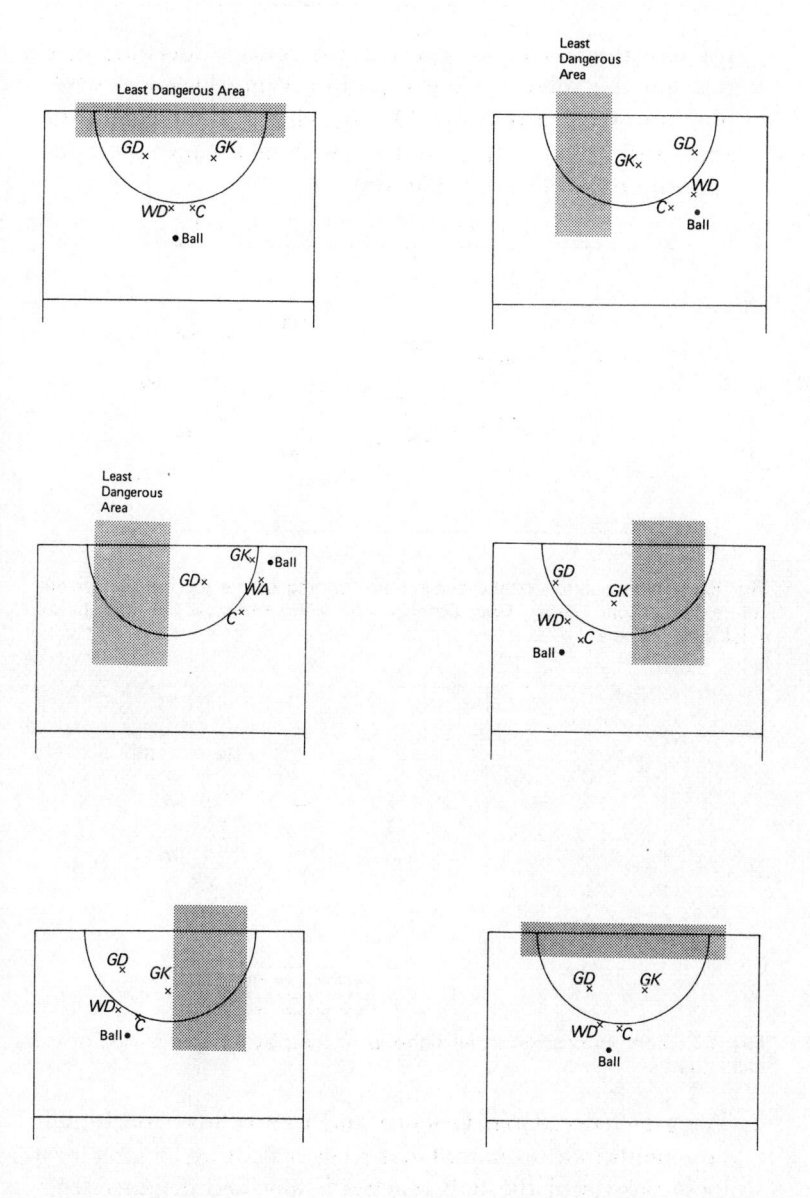

Fig. 61a–f Examples of the zone moving in relationship to the ball. The shaded areas indicate the territory away from the immediate concentration of play and so relatively unimportant. If a pass is made into any of these areas it usually has to be a long high one giving defences time to move and intercept

82 Defending Tactics

prepare themselves to travel down court to defend; they take on the roles of Centre and/or Wing Defence, while play is in the centre court. On the whistle, Centre joins the zone and Wing Attack and Goal Attack cause as much opposition as they can. (Fig. 62)

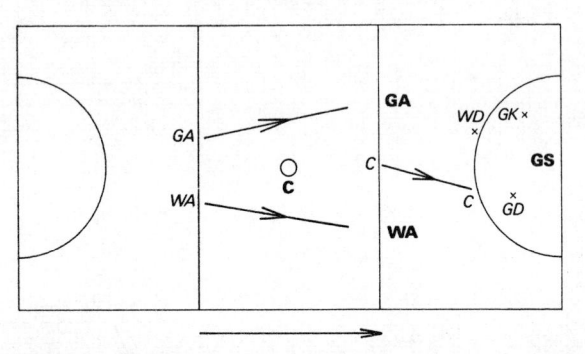

Fig. 62 Three-quarters of the circle zone forming before the whistle for the centre pass; Goal Keeper, Goal Defence and Wing Defence. Centre joins as quickly as possible

Goalkeeper, goal defence, wing defence and centre forming a zone in relationship to the position of the ball.

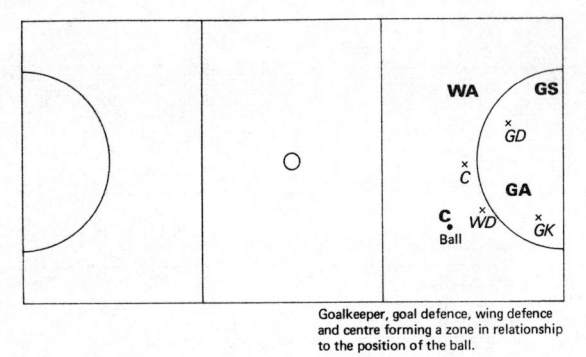

Fig. 63 Zone in position in relationship to the player in possession of the ball—Centre

2. Wing Defence, Goal Defence and Centre may mark their opponents man-to-man, Goal Keeper floating looking for a loose pass until the ball reaches a specified distance from goal (this is often shortly after the ball enters the attacking third of the court or when it is approximately half way down the attacking third), at which point the players involved in the zone drop back into position. Because of the

territorial restrictions, Goal Keeper in this instance, has only a slight chance of an interception before the zone forms.

The zone attempts to maintain its unity while continually moving to cover any possible route to goal along which the attackers may play the ball. (Fig. 63)

One of the ways recommended to beat a zone defence, is for the attacking players to receive the ball as close to the defenders as possible, so forcing them to move back to the stipulated three feet. If therefore it is felt necessary Wing Defence and Centre may choose to make their contribution to the zone at a distance of three feet from the circle edge. (Fig. 64) However, my view is that the front part of the zone should function

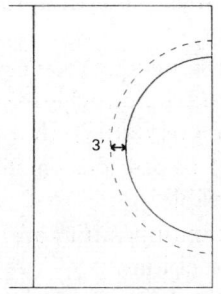

Fig. 64 Wing Defence and Centre describing their arc three feet from the shooting circle

approximately a foot from the circle edge so allowing some room for manoeuvrability and pre-supposing that any ball being passed too close to the circle will be intercepted. (Fig. 65) Each team will decide from which position they have most success.

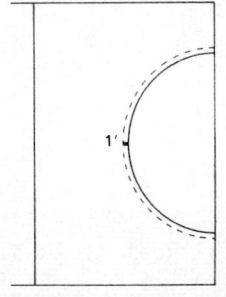

Fig. 65 Arc from the shooting circle at a distance of only one foot

SUMMARY

Whenever defensive play is needed, it should not be forgotten that for the most part one's aim is to regain possession of the ball; that the strongest weapon is that of surprise; and that the surest means of defence is undoubtedly to attack.

At every possible opportunity a defender plays to counteract favourable attacking situations by:
1. Preventing the attacks feeding from the circle edge, and from the centre front.
2. Trying to congest the space that the attacks attempt to create.
3. Not responding the same way to every situation.
4. Restricting vision and action wherever possible.
5. Breaking any rhythm or pattern that may be established.
6. Trying to force long passes, so that the ball is in the air for the longest time possible.
7. Taking time from the opposition and trying to force them into making hasty decisions.
8. Whenever possible taking the initiative and answering problem with problem.

Conclusion

As with all ball games, it is the constantly changing pattern and the unpredictability of procedure that makes netball a challenge, and these same factors make tactical preparations interesting.

To permutate for every eventuality would be impossible— for which I'm grateful, because if this were possible there would be little left to exercise the thinking player. It is hoped that the suggestions put forward might serve as a foundation for understanding and as a framework around which others may explore and develop their own ideas.

In this book, I have attempted to clarify my own views on the issue. I have proposed a system whereby the team may be unified without being restricted, informed without being confused and, although directed towards co-operation, are allowed opportunities to use initiative and flair.

It is hoped that the book will prove an acceptable and unpretentious guide and reference in its own right; but if it serves to promote some thinking, and a possible challenge of accepted views by netball enthusiasts, it will not have failed in its objectives.

11+ Confidence

CEM-Style Practice Exam Papers

Book

2

The Eureka! 11+ Confidence series
Practice Exam Papers covering multiple disciplines:
Comprehension, Verbal Reasoning,
Non-Verbal Reasoning and Numerical Reasoning

Numerical Reasoning: Advanced Training Workbooks
Tough exam paper questions and detailed explanations of how to tackle them, to increase speed and reduce error.

Verbal Reasoning: Advanced Training Workbooks
The *1000-Word Brain Boost* is a powerful, intensive course teaching Synonyms, Antonyms, Odd-One-Out, Analogy, Vocabulary and Cloze in modern multiple-choice questions. Its famous *Explanations* section explains hundreds of language subtleties and distinctions that many 11+ candidates find challenging.

Non-Verbal Reasoning: The *Non-Verbal Ninja* Training Course
The *Non-Verbal Ninja* is an intensive *visual* course for core exam skills. The set of 3 training workbooks include over 600 puzzles coupled with *visual* explanations. They build both fundamental skills and the crucial confidence to seek out rules without having to have them explained first. Each book rapidly moves on from simple levels to challenging training puzzles that enhance the capacities of even the strongest 11+ hopefuls.

Please check the website www.eureka11plus.org/updates for updates and clarifications to this book.

Copyright © Eureka! Eleven Plus 2016, 2017, 2018
Best-selling, realistic, 11+ exam preparation series

Revised 1 May 2018
Published in the United Kingdom by:
Eureka! Eleven Plus Exams · Website: http://www.eureka11plus.org · Email: office@eureka11plus.org

The moral right of the authors has been asserted. All rights reserved. Without limiting the rights under copyright reserved above no part of this publication may be reproduced, stored or introduced into a retrieval system, or transmitted, in any form or by any means without the prior written permission of the copyright owner of this book. Eureka! Eleven Plus Exams provides these resources as an educational tool for children and their teachers, to develop and consolidate key skills. Eureka! Eleven Plus Exams is not associated with the CEM. CEM is a trademark of the Centre for Evaluation and Monitoring, a part of Durham University. The practice exam papers from Eureka! Eleven Plus Exams are not produced by, associated with, endorsed by, or otherwise linked to the CEM of Durham University.

Eureka! Eleven Plus is grateful to Amy Francis for her assistance.

ISBN-13: 978-1718864368
ISBN-10: 1718864361

We are all human and vulnerable to error. Eureka! Eleven Plus is very grateful to any reader who notifies us on office@eureka11plus.org of an unnoticed error, so we can immediately correct it and provide a tangible reward.

Helping your child gain confidence through practice

As the 11+ Examination approaches, it is vital to practice Exam Paper questions, but with limited time available it is equally important for the process itself to build the fund of knowledge and skills. Time is scarce, exam styles are continually changing and solid information can seem elusive.

There is a trend towards multiple choice formats that are quick and cheap to mark. Pupils need experience in deciding and documenting their choices rapidly and clearly. Pupils also need the confidence that comes from familiarity with questions couched in this way, and with the layout of question papers and response sheets. Wise parents recognise that pupils also need to focus on aspects they find difficult, and need guidance when they get stuck or make mistakes.

The *Eureka! 11+ Confidence* series of Exam Papers provides exactly this:

- Question papers laid out in modern, multiple-choice format, as used by CEM and others.
- Answer sheets laid out in modern format (in places requiring digit-by-digit entry)
- Full answers with explanations
- Supplementary books giving very detailed methods, tips and tricks on the more challenging aspects of Numerical Reasoning and focussed training on Verbal Reasoning

In supporting your child's preparation for the exam:

- Do as much exam paper practice as possible. The variety of material helps retain attention.
- Cut out the multiple choice answer sheet and use it to record the answers. By making the experience as authentic as possible, you will reduce exam-day anxiety.
- Carry out the practice exams formally: pupil seated alone, away from *any* distractions.
- Give no help (nor encouragement) during their timed attempt at the paper.
- Immediately after the paper, encourage the pupil to mark their own work. Immediacy and involvement increase interest and enjoyment in exam preparation.
- Insist on discussing the questions which were not answered correctly. Do not set aside any errors as "silly mistakes". All mistakes are silly. The key to 11+ is attention to seemingly small details.

The learning from Exam Paper practice arises not only through gaining familiarity with the design and layout of Exam Papers, but also through enhancing the fundamental skills which are being tested. Underline the importance of learning how errors were made and how they may be prevented in future. Tips, tricks and (most of all) systematic approaches for avoiding the major traps at 11+ are given in the associated "*Eureka! Challenging Maths and Numerical Reasoning Exam Questions for 11+*" series of books. An efficient tool for concentrated enhancement of synonyms, antonyms, vocabulary and cloze (complete-the-sentence) is the *1000 Word Brain Boost* series.

Thoughtful support from parents can be crucial for pupils in the run-up to examinations. Use the Eureka! Practice Exam Papers, with the *Numerical Reasoning* advanced training and *Brain Boost* vocabulary training books, to help them reach their full potential.

Using this book to practice for your 11+

Make the practice as real as possible, to get the most benefit.

Cut out the answer sheet so that you do not have to flick back and forth.

Find a place where you will be undisturbed for 45 minutes.

Ensure the background is quiet: no TV, radio, computer, music or chat.

Do not get help or encouragement from anyone while you are doing the timed exam.

Immediately after answering the paper, mark yourself using the answers at the back.

Where you made a mistake, or got stuck, read the explanation and discuss with your parent or teacher. It may seem embarrassing to discuss a mistake but your success depends on you thinking carefully about each mistake and improving your methods so that you make fewer in future.

Do as much exam paper practice as you can.

If you are finding it difficult to answer the Numerical Reasoning questions correctly, use the *Eureka! Maths and Numerical Reasoning* workbooks which give detailed methods, tips and tricks through worked examples on difficult questions designed to maximise your learning. Focused training in difficult vocabulary, synonyms and antonyms can be obtained in the *1000 Word Brain Boost* training workbooks.

Exam instructions may be similar to those shown below. You may also get instructions played from a recording or read out.

Instructions you may receive in the 11+ Exam

Enter your personal details onto the answer sheet.

Do all your working in the question book.

Write your answers on the answer sheet, as only this will be marked.

Each paper consists of a series of sections which may have individual time limits.

Sections may begin with an example. You can refer back to the examples as often as you wish.

Before each section you may be told the time allowed and the number of questions in that section.

Answer as many questions as you can. If you come across a question you cannot answer, move on to the next question.

There is no negative marking. Incorrect answers score nothing.

If you have time left at the end of a section, go back and answer any questions you have missed, but only within that same section.

E

Non-Verbal Reasoning

1. A B C D E F
2. A B C D E F
3. A B C D E F
4. A B C D E F
5. A B C D E F
6. A B C D E F
7. A B C D E F
8. A B C D E F
9. A B C D E F
10. A B C D E F

Numerical Reasoning Part A

1. A B C D E
2. A B C D E
3. A B C D E
4. A B C D E
5. A B C D E
6. A B C D E
7. A B C D E
8. A B C D E
9. A B C D E
10. A B C D E

Numerical Reasoning Part B

1. [ ][ ] 0-9 / 0-9
2. [ ][ ] 0-9 / 0-9
3. [ ][ ] 0-9 / 0-9
4. [ ][ ] 0-9 / 0-9
5. [ ][ ] 0-9 / 0-9
6. [ ][ ] 0-9 / 0-9
7. [ ][ ] 0-9 / 0-9
8. [ ][ ] 0-9 / 0-9
9. [ ][ ] 0-9 / 0-9
10. [ ][ ] 0-9 / 0-9
11. [ ][ ] 0-9 / 0-9
12. [ ][ ] 0-9 / 0-9
13. [ ][ ] 0-9 / 0-9

Similar Words

1. A B C D E
2. A B C D E
3. A B C D E
4. A B C D E
5. A B C D E
6. A B C D E
7. A B C D E
8. A B C D E
9. A B C D E
10. A B C D E
11. A B C D E
12. A B C D E
13. A B C D E
14. A B C D E
15. A B C D E
16. A B C D E
17. A B C D E
18. A B C D E
19. A B C D E
20. A B C D E
21. A B C D E
22. A B C D E
23. A B C D E
24. A B C D E
25. A B C D E
26. A B C D E
27. A B C D E

Find the Missing Words

1. A B C D E
2. A B C D E
3. A B C D E
4. A B C D E
5. A B C D E
6. A B C D E
7. A B C D E
8. A B C D E
9. A B C D E
10. A B C D E
11. A B C D E
12. A B C D E
13. A B C D E
14. A B C D E
15. A B C D E
16. A B C D E

F

Analogies

1. A B C D E
2. A B C D E
3. A B C D E
4. A B C D E
5. A B C D E
6. A B C D E
7. A B C D E
8. A B C D E

Shuffled Sentences

1. A B C D E
2. A B C D E
3. A B C D E
4. A B C D E
5. A B C D E
6. A B C D E
7. A B C D E
8. A B C D E

Comprehension

1. A B C D
2. A B C D
3. A B C D
4. A B C D
5. A B C D
6. A B C D
7. A B C D
8. A B C D
9. A B C D
10. A B C D
11. A B C D
12. A B C D
13. A B C D
14. A B C D
15. A B C D
16. A B C D
17. A B C D
18. A B C D
19. A B C D
20. A B C D
21. A B C D
22. A B C D
23. A B C D

Numerical Reasoning Part A

1. A B C D E
2. A B C D E
3. A B C D E
4. A B C D E
5. A B C D E
6. A B C D E
7. A B C D E
8. A B C D E

Non-Verbal Reasoning

1. A B C D E F
2. A B C D E F
3. A B C D E F
4. A B C D E F
5. A B C D E F
6. A B C D E F
7. A B C D E F
8. A B C D E F
9. A B C D E F
10. A B C D E F
11. A B C D E F
12. A B C D E F
13. A B C D E F
14. A B C D E F
15. A B C D E F
16. A B C D E F

Numerical Reasoning Part B

1. ☐☐ 0-9 0-9
2. ☐☐ 0-9 0-9
3. ☐☐ 0-9 0-9
4. ☐☐ 0-9 0-9
5. ☐☐ 0-9 0-9
6. ☐☐ 0-9 0-9
7. ☐☐ 0-9 0-9
8. ☐☐ 0-9 0-9

G

Numerical Reasoning

1	A	B	C	D	E	F	G	H	I	J
2	A	B	C	D	E	F	G	H	I	J
3	A	B	C	D	E	F	G	H	I	J
4	A	B	C	D	E	F	G	H	I	J
5	A	B	C	D	E	F	G	H	I	J
6	A	B	C	D	E	F	G	H	I	J
7	A	B	C	D	E	F	G	H	I	J
8	A	B	C	D	E	F	G	H	I	J
9	A	B	C	D	E	F	G	H	I	J
10	A	B	C	D	E	F	G	H	I	J
11	A	B	C	D	E	F	G	H	I	J
12	A	B	C	D	E	F	G	H	I	J
13	A	B	C	D	E	F	G	H	I	J
14	A	B	C	D	E	F	G	H	I	J
15	A	B	C	D	E	F	G	H	I	J
16	A	B	C	D	E	F	G	H	I	J
17	A	B	C	D	E	F	G	H	I	J
18	A	B	C	D	E	F	G	H	I	J

Non-Verbal Reasoning

1	A	B	C	D	E	F
2	A	B	C	D	E	F
3	A	B	C	D	E	F
4	A	B	C	D	E	F
5	A	B	C	D	E	F
6	A	B	C	D	E	F
7	A	B	C	D	E	F
8	A	B	C	D	E	F
9	A	B	C	D	E	F
10	A	B	C	D	E	F
11	A	B	C	D	E	F
12	A	B	C	D	E	F
13	A	B	C	D	E	F

Find the Missing Word

1	A	B	C	D	E
2	A	B	C	D	E
3	A	B	C	D	E
4	A	B	C	D	E
5	A	B	C	D	E
6	A	B	C	D	E
7	A	B	C	D	E
8	A	B	C	D	E
9	A	B	C	D	E
10	A	B	C	D	E
11	A	B	C	D	E
12	A	B	C	D	E
13	A	B	C	D	E
14	A	B	C	D	E
15	A	B	C	D	E
16	A	B	C	D	E
17	A	B	C	D	E
18	A	B	C	D	E
19	A	B	C	D	E
20	A	B	C	D	E
21	A	B	C	D	E
22	A	B	C	D	E
23	A	B	C	D	E

Groups

1	A	B	C	D	E
2	A	B	C	D	E
3	A	B	C	D	E
4	A	B	C	D	E
5	A	B	C	D	E
6	A	B	C	D	E
7	A	B	C	D	E
8	A	B	C	D	E
9	A	B	C	D	E
10	A	B	C	D	E
11	A	B	C	D	E
12	A	B	C	D	E
13	A	B	C	D	E
14	A	B	C	D	E
15	A	B	C	D	E
16	A	B	C	D	E
17	A	B	C	D	E
18	A	B	C	D	E
19	A	B	C	D	E
20	A	B	C	D	E
21	A	B	C	D	E
22	A	B	C	D	E
23	A	B	C	D	E
24	A	B	C	D	E
25	A	B	C	D	E
26	A	B	C	D	E
27	A	B	C	D	E
28	A	B	C	D	E

H

Shuffled Sentences

1. A B C D E
2. A B C D E
3. A B C D E
4. A B C D E
5. A B C D E
6. A B C D E
7. A B C D E
8. A B C D E

Non-Verbal Reasoning

1. A B C D E F
2. A B C D E F
3. A B C D E F
4. A B C D E F
5. A B C D E F
6. A B C D E F
7. A B C D E F
8. A B C D E F
9. A B C D E F

Comprehension

1. A B C D
2. A B C D
3. A B C D
4. A B C D
5. A B C D
6. A B C D
7. A B C D
8. A B C D
9. A B C D
10. A B C D
11. A B C D
12. A B C D

Find the Missing Word

1. A B C D E
2. A B C D E
3. A B C D E
4. A B C D E
5. A B C D E
6. A B C D E
7. A B C D E
8. A B C D E

Numerical Reasoning

1. A B C D E F G H I J
2. A B C D E F G H I J
3. A B C D E F G H I J
4. A B C D E F G H I J
5. A B C D E F G H I J
6. A B C D E F G H I J
7. A B C D E F G H I J
8. A B C D E F G H I J
9. A B C D E F G H I J
10. A B C D E F G H I J
11. A B C D E F G H I J
12. A B C D E F G H I J
13. A B C D E F G H I J
14. A B C D E F G H I J
15. A B C D E F G H I J
16. A B C D E F G H I J
17. A B C D E F G H I J
18. A B C D E F G H I J

Similar Words

1. A B C D E
2. A B C D E
3. A B C D E
4. A B C D E
5. A B C D E
6. A B C D E
7. A B C D E
8. A B C D E
9. A B C D E
10. A B C D E
11. A B C D E
12. A B C D E
13. A B C D E
14. A B C D E
15. A B C D E
16. A B C D E
17. A B C D E
18. A B C D E
19. A B C D E
20. A B C D E

Paper E

Non-verbal Reasoning

In each group of pictures on the left, one is missing, shown by a question mark. Choose the picture on the right that is best suited to be the missing picture. Shade your answer on the answer sheet by choosing one of the options A to F.

You have 6 minutes to answer the questions in this section.

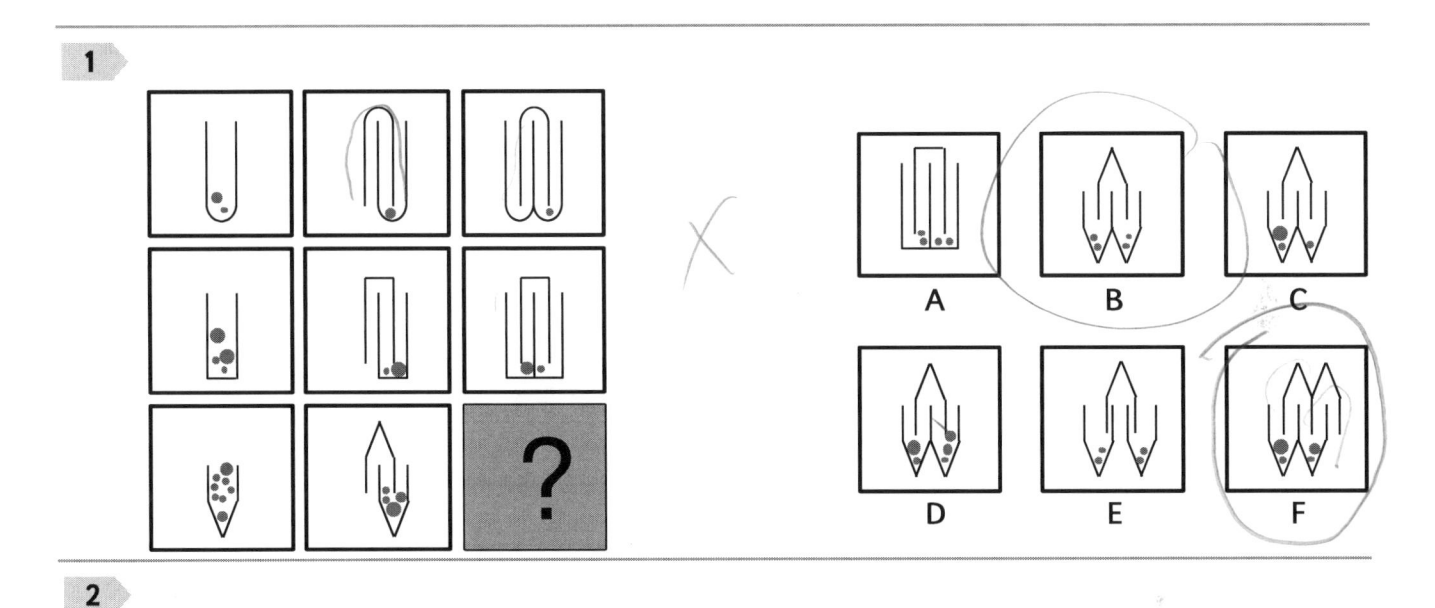

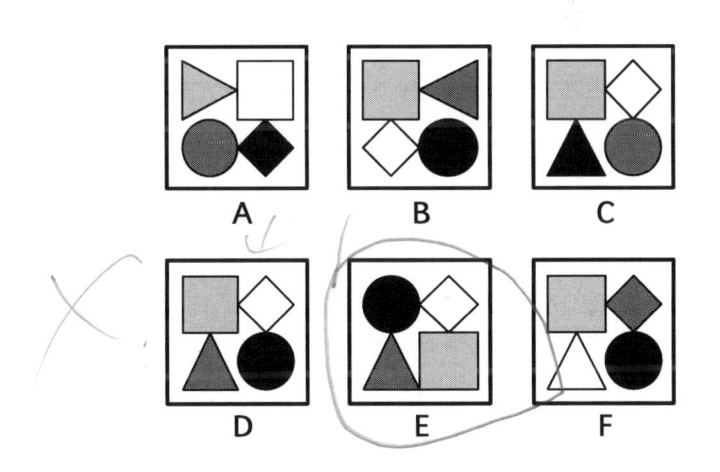

1

2

▶ Please continue to the following page

Non-verbal Reasoning

3

4

5

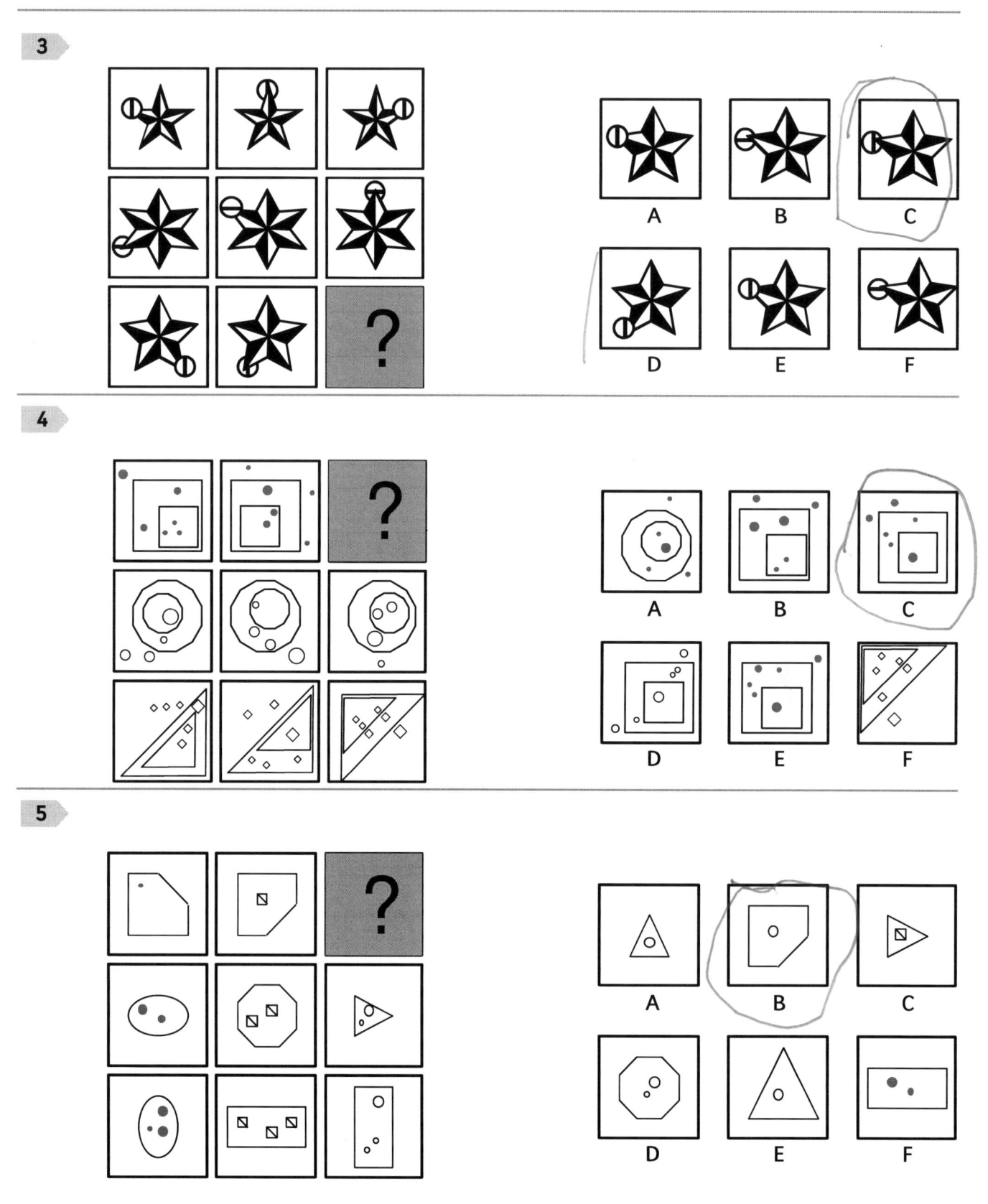

▶ Please continue to the following page

Non-verbal Reasoning

Paper **E** Page 3

6

7

8

▶ Please continue to the following page

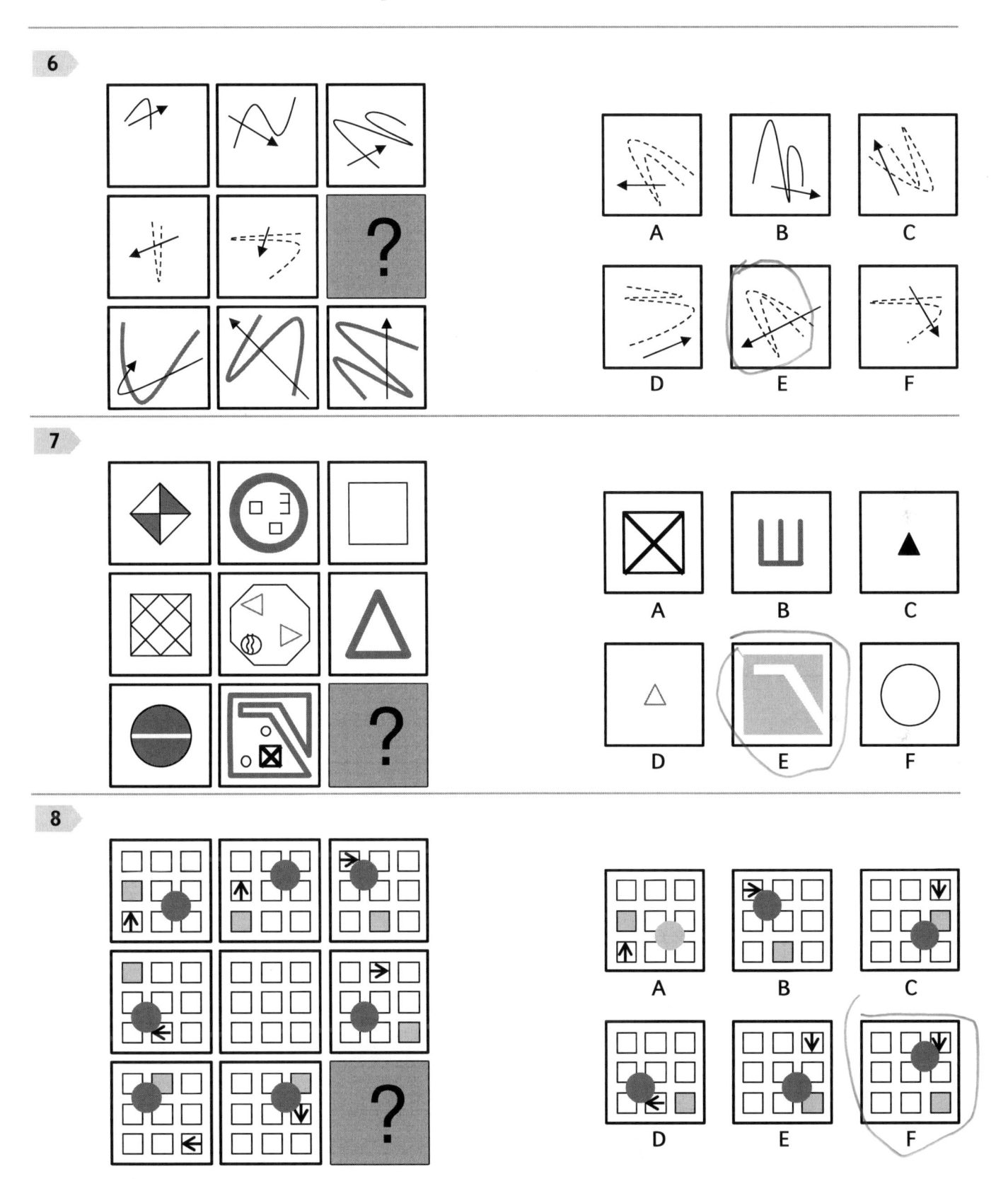

Non-verbal Reasoning

Paper **E** Page **4**

9

10

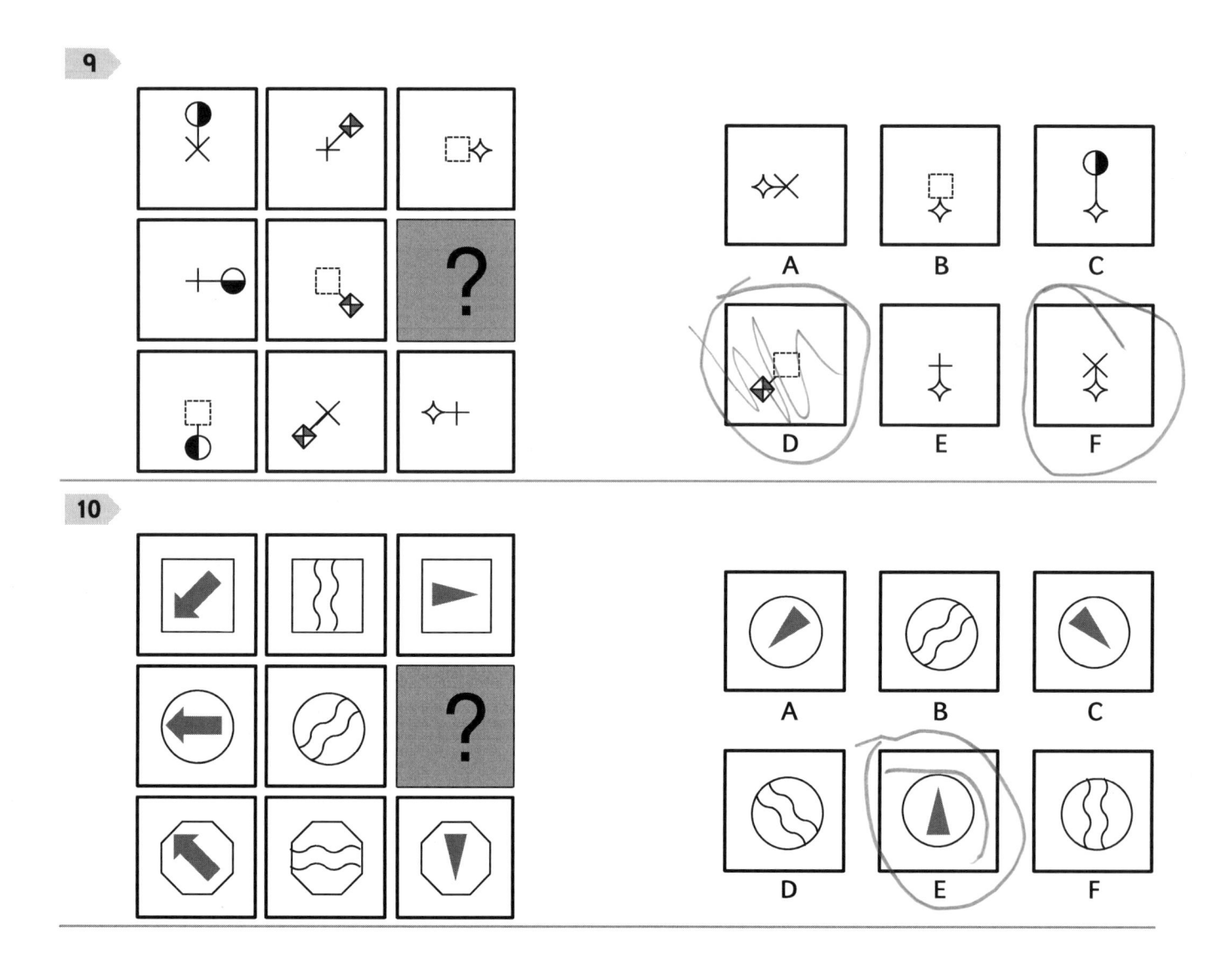

This is the end of this section. If time remains, check your answers in this section only.

Numerical Reasoning Part A

Numerical Reasoning Part A

In each of the questions, choose the correct answer option and shade it on your answer sheet.
You have 7 minutes to answer the questions in this section.

1

Seven children pick strawberries, collecting 231 altogether. They share them equally. Three of the children are sisters, and decide to pool their strawberries to take them home in one large bag. How many strawberries will they put in that bag?

A	B	C	D	E
21	23	33	99	123

2

Alec saves £4 per week from the pocket money he receives at the end of each week. He wants to buy a model aeroplane for £70. If he starts saving now, at the start of a week, how many weeks will it be before he has saved enough money to buy the aeroplane?

A	B	C	D	E
17	18	66	70	280

3

Which one of these five prize amounts is the median?

A	B	C	D	E
one third of one hundred pounds	½ of £60	a 3×3 grid of plates, each containing three £1 coins	3 £10 notes and 3 £1 coins	£8, doubled, and doubled again

4

After a wonderful restaurant meal, the three friends decided to add a generous tip to the £39 bill, so that they each contributed £17 to the total payment. How much was the tip?

A	B	C	D	E
2	12	19	20	21

▶ Please continue to the following page

Numerical Reasoning Part A

5

The overnight train promised to be exciting, with a bunk bed and fancy furnishings, but how long would the journey take, if it began at 22:30 and finished at a quarter past 6 in the morning?

A	B	C	D	E
5.75 hours	6 hours	7 hours 15 min	7 ½ hours	7 hours 45 min

6

If the distance they travelled was 310 km, what was their average speed on the journey?

A	B	C	D	E
40 km/hour	51 km/hour	62 km/hour	75 km/hour	77 ½ km/hour

7

Of 250 people squeezed in a concert hall, half were men. Forty percent of the people bought popcorn. What is the range of possible numbers of men who bought popcorn (smallest to largest)?

A	B	C	D	E
100 to 175	75 to 125	40 to 210	125 to 150	0 to 100

"These chocolate sticks are marvellously tasty, and hardly any Calories!" enthused Lucille. "Even though it says they are 450 Calories per 100g, the box contains only 40g of them."

8 How many Calories are in one boxful of chocolate sticks?

A	B	C	D	E
40	18	180	80	45

9 What percentage of the 2000 Calories a day Lucille allowed herself would one box be?

A	B	C	D	E
4%	4.5%	9%	18%	45%

10 "And they are a bargain," said the shopkeeper. "£0.99 per box, or £3 for 5 boxes."

How much money would Lucille save by buying the 5-box deal rather than 5 separate boxes?

A	B	C	D	E
£1.95	£2.10	£2	£2.97	£3

✗ This is the end of this section. If time remains, check your answers in this section only.

Numerical Reasoning Part B

Numerical Reasoning Part B

Write the two digits, one in each box. Put a zero in the first box if your answer is less than 10. Shade one box in each column, corresponding to the digits.

You have 10 minutes to answer the questions in this section.

1

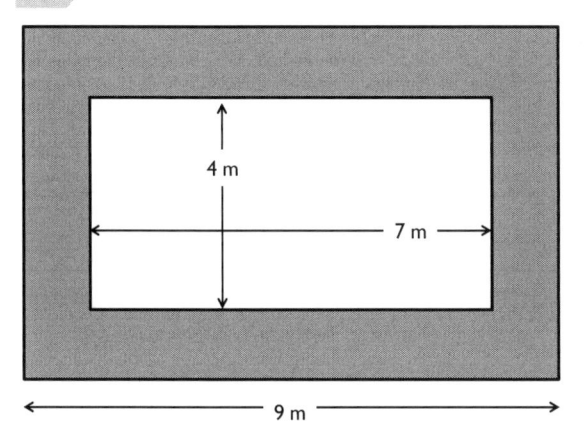

The Nawab of Shirazpur was delighted with the gigantic painting prepared for his great hall, but he also wants an enormous golden frame (shaded in this sketch) to go around it, giving an equal-sized border on all four sides.

How tall is the frame in metres, from top to bottom?

(Diagram shows outer rectangle 9 m wide with inner rectangle 7 m wide and 4 m tall)

2 To put silver braid around the outer rim of the frame, how many metres of braid are needed?

3 What is the shaded area of the golden frame, in square metres?

Relocating the Zebulon Zoo is a traumatic task. One hundred and twenty animals still await transport, and they belong to five species. The numbers of three species that will travel in today's convoy are shown in this table.

Animal	Number
Hippopotamus	32
Zebra	
Rhinoceros	12
Giraffe	
Elephant	13

4 The giraffes and zebras will travel in tomorrow's convoy. How many animals will be in tomorrow's convoy?

5 The giraffes outnumber the zebras 2:1. How many giraffes are there?

6

Farmer Nelda buys 500 kg of grain for her flock of 15 sheep. Each sheep eats 800 g of grain per day. For how many days can she fully feed her flock? (Do not count any final day where there is not enough grain to feed the whole flock).

| **Note:** | 1 kg = 1000 g | 1 kilogram = 1000 grams |

▶ Please continue to the following page

Numerical Reasoning Part B

"Everyone says there's no need to practice for this exam," complained Griselda. "I don't care if I scored low on these two practice papers, it is only the real exam that counts."

"But I increased my score enormously. This could help you a lot," replied Tabitha, pressing into her best friend's reluctant hands the other practice books.

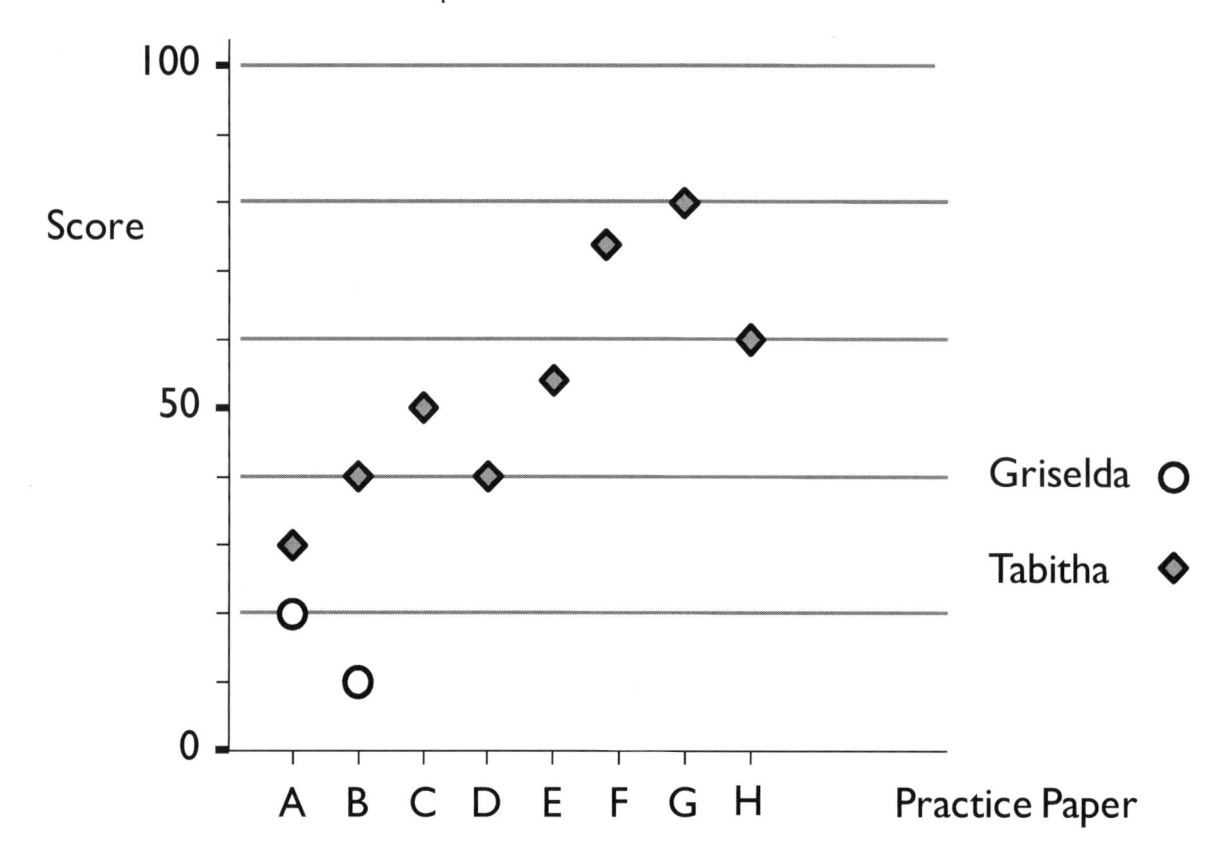

7

What was Tabitha's average score on paper C and paper D?

8

On paper A, how much higher was Tabitha's score than Griselda's?

9

If, from paper A to paper H, Griselda increases her score by the same number of points as Tabitha does, how much will Griselda score on paper H?

▶ Please continue to the following page

Numerical Reasoning Part B

By the end of a day at the market, Violet had managed to sell all of the two dozen phone chargers at £5 each, having bought them for £3 each.

10

How many pounds had Violet spent on buying the phone chargers?

Scarves, her other product, had fared less well. At first she sold only half of the dozen, at £10 each, and had to later slash her price to sell the rest at £5 each, just the price she had originally paid for them.

11

In total, how many pounds had she sold her entire batch of scarves for?

12

What was her total profit that day?

13

This shape has mirror symmetry in two axes. What is its perimeter, in m?

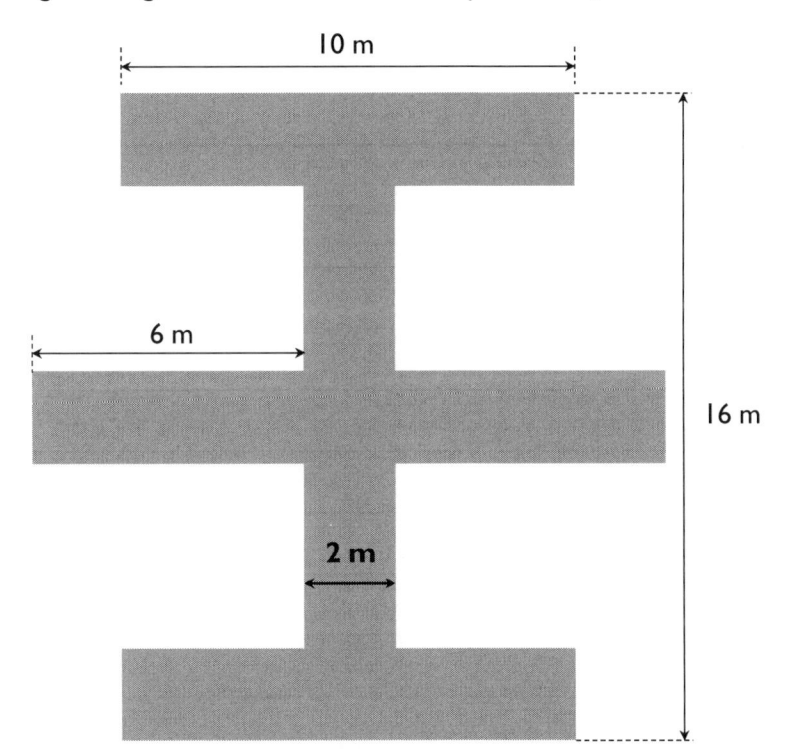

10 m
6 m
16 m
2 m

❌ **This is the end of this section. If time remains, check your answers in this section only.**

Similar Words

Paper **E** Page **10**

Similar Words

Identify which word is MOST SIMILAR in meaning to the word on the left. Each question has only one correct answer. For each question shade your one chosen answer on the answer sheet.

You have **12** minutes to answer the questions in this section.

1 dexterity

A	B	C	D	E
outsides	simultaneity	structure	skill	region

2 reported

A	B	C	D	E
document	described	incident	stating	assertion

3 steal

A	B	C	D	E
metal	flair	iron	design	loot

4 eloquent

A	B	C	D	E
persuasive	watery	confusing	often	insufficient

5 member

A	B	C	D	E
fracture	captain	recall	part	team

6 folk

A	B	C	D	E
implement	singers	divide	song	people

7 semblance

A	B	C	D	E
hug	displayed	veneer	cavort	peek

8 staff

A	B	C	D	E
customer	squeeze	proprietor	rigid	rod

▶ Please continue to the following page

Similar Words

		A	B	C	D	E
9	chevron	knight	arrow	helicopter	horse	sharp

		A	B	C	D	E
10	blush	verdant	shrub	azure	flush	hurry

		A	B	C	D	E
11	stony	sympathetic	ancient	rugged	heated	fiction

		A	B	C	D	E
12	upended	finalised	awaited	dangled	dazzled	inverted

		A	B	C	D	E
13	rapier	singer	sword	criminal	knocker	closure

		A	B	C	D	E
14	slip	cut	slash	sliding	mouth	mistake

		A	B	C	D	E
15	elongate	delay	express	stretch	entrance	pigtail

		A	B	C	D	E
16	quench	princess	damsel	spanner	satisfy	grip

		A	B	C	D	E
17	melodramatic	cool	showy	unruffled	immediate	mottled

		A	B	C	D	E
18	paramount	supreme	immobile	hilly	horse	insufficient

▶ Please continue to the following page

Similar Words

		A	B	C	D	E
19	isolate	disrespect	detach	unpunctual	heat	delay

		A	B	C	D	E
20	spike	addressed	related	omit	indicate	prong

		A	B	C	D	E
21	accommodate	dislike	punctuate	schedule	house	angle

		A	B	C	D	E
22	entertain	transport	amuse	access	invade	landscape

		A	B	C	D	E
23	granule	pellet	ancestor	ruler	regulation	marking

		A	B	C	D	E
24	previous	expensive	severe	cunning	earlier	secret

		A	B	C	D	E
25	nobility	talent	flexibility	capacity	relocation	grandeur

		A	B	C	D	E
26	glean	tidy	gather	tilt	joyous	slender

		A	B	C	D	E
27	drench	tear	moist	wrest	soak	farm

This is the end of this section. If time remains, check your answers in this section only.

Find the Missing Words

Find the Missing Words

In each of the following sentences, one or two words are missing.

Complete the sentence by choosing one word from the choices A to E. Mark your answer on the answer sheet.

You have 10 minutes to answer the questions in this section.

Example

A	B	C	D	E
drought	wind	rain	warm	changeable

The gentle shower of rain was very welcome after so many weeks of [Example].

The correct answer is A. Mark it as shown here:

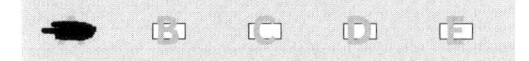

Question 1

A	B	C	D	E
cures	coarse	covers	course	cores

This was not the delicate, sophisticated fabric she had wanted to envelop her pillows: it was [Question 1] material with ugly stripes.

Question 2

A	B	C	D	E
hidden	hanger	arched	hangar	holding

A shaft of summer sunlight cut through the [Question 2] as its giant doors opened, revealing the top secret helicopter to the select group of military dignitaries.

Question 3

A	B	C	D	E
tale	lore	law	tail	tile

The story of the love-struck couple who eloped in a riverboat is an established part of local [Question 3].

▶ Please continue to the following page

Find the Missing Words

Question 4

A	B	C	D	E
halter	alter	all	altar	alder

"What's done is done, and I cannot [Question 4] it," he confided to the priest.

Questions 5 and 6

A	B	C	D	E
council	console	counsel	conceal	cancel

They were glad to receive good [Question 5] for the difficult decision on whether to [Question 6] the development of the new machine after all that investment.

Questions 7 and 8

A	B	C	D	E
vein	envelop	vain	envelope	vane

Realising too late the seriousness of the warning letter she had ignored earlier, she struggled in [Question 7] as the fake doctor's mysterious drug flowed into her body and a warm stupor began to [Question 8] her.

Question 9

A	B	C	D	E
parents	parent	parented	parents'	parent's

"It is because this meeting is designed for all of you that we call it the [Question 9] evening," announced the head teacher.

▶ Please continue to the following page

Find the Missing Words

Question 10

A	B	C	D	E
escalate	aspect	accept	except	expect

Nearly tripping over herself with delight, Alexandra climbed the podium to [Question 10] the award.

Question 11

A	B	C	D	E
affect	afflict	infect	effect	inflict

Susanna tried very hard to ensure that the accident she witnessed did not [Question 11] her performance in the exam.

Question 12

A	B	C	D	E
thorough	throw	threw	though	through

After his teacher warned him about his careless mistakes, Peter made sure his checking was [Question 12].

▶ Please continue to the next page

Find the Missing Words

Questions 13 and 14

A	B	C	D	E
compliant	complement	complaint	compliment	complete

"Every time he calls us, it is with a [Question 13] about our hotel," bemoaned the receptionist, "Can't he think of even one single [Question 14]?"

Questions 15 and 16

A	B	C	D	E
corral	chorale	curl	coral	choral

The usher hurried through the gardens, trying to [Question 15] all the guests into the great hall for the [Question 16] evening."

This is the end of this test. If time remains, check your answers in this section only.

Paper F

Analogies

Examine the relationship between the first pair of words. Then look at the next word and identify which of the options A to E produces a second pair with a relationship best matching the first. Each question has only one correct answer. For each question shade your one chosen answer on the answer sheet.

You have 5 minutes to answer the questions in this section.

Example

Man is to woman as fox is to

A	B	C	D	E
child	boy	pregnant	mare	vixen

The correct answer is E. Mark it on the answer sheet as shown below.

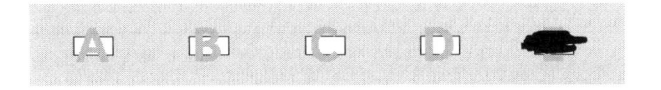

Achievement is to reward as crime is to

A	B	C	D	E
loot	getaway	jewellery	penalty	capture

1

Newspaper is to read as sandwich is to

A	B	C	D	E
bread	ham	see	eaten	made

2

Europe is to Sweden as Asia is to

A	B	C	D	E
Japan	Peking	Baghdad	France	Atlantic

3

▶ Please continue to the following page

Analogies

All is to many as none is to

A	B	C	D	E
rarely	empty	infrequently	vanished	few

4

Architect is to skyscrapers as sculptor is to

A	B	C	D	E
wax	statue	art	chisel	wood

5

Cool is to cold as old is to

A	B	C	D	E
aged	oldest	historical	ancient	told

6

Gift is to presenting as secret is to

A	B	C	D	E
concealed	fallacy	past	future	confiding

7

Hospital is to patients as museum is to

A	B	C	D	E
dinosaurs	visitors	paintings	guides	statues

8

This is the end of this section. If time remains, check your answers in this section only.

Shuffled Sentences

Shuffled Sentences

Each sentence has had its words shuffled and an additional word inserted. Identify the additional word. Mark the option A to E on your answer sheet.

You have **6** minutes to answer the questions in this section.

1

had miss what she never has cannot one one

A	B	C	D	E
cannot	never	miss	she	one

2

a can sorry regret of a moment's save reflection lifetime

A	B	C	D	E
can	of	save	regret	sorry

3

they through sun until night danced the daybreak

A	B	C	D	E
sun	daybreak	they	until	the

▶ Please continue to the following page

Shuffled Sentences

4

king dishonesty a land away far lies in dying the

A	B	C	D	E
dishonesty	king	lies	far	in

5

up must that they come down say goes they what

A	B	C	D	E
what	they	say	must	come

6

I invite both of party to birthday wonderful us please your

A	B	C	D	E
both	wonderful	I	invite	party

7

monster to face finally face with to began the crying george tremble

A	B	C	D	E
monster	face	began	to	crying

8

sign the letter only low dam the was about to a was that rumbling burst

A	B	C	D	E
to	sign	was	a	letter

This is the end of this section. If time remains, check your answers in this section only.

Comprehension

Comprehension

There are two passages below, each with a set of questions after it.

Read each passage below and then answer the questions that follow. Indicate your answer by shading one of the choices A to D.

You have a *total* of 17 minutes to answer *all* the questions in this section. Remember that this includes *two* separate passages.

Three weeks later, Spayley the advertising expert informed the world of the coming of a new breakfast food, heralded under the resounding name of "Filboid Studge." He put forth no pictures of massive babies expanded with fungus-like rapidity under its forcing influence, or of representatives of the world's leading nations scrambling eagerly for its possession. One huge sombre poster depicted the Damned in Hell suffering a new torment from their inability to get at the Filboid Studge. Elegant young fiends held it in transparent bowls just beyond their reach.

The scene was rendered even more gruesome by a subtle suggestion of the features of leading men and women of the day in the portrayal of the Lost Souls. Prominent individuals of all political parties, society hostesses, well-known dramatic authors and novelists, and distinguished aviators were dimly recognizable in that doomed throng. Noted lights of the musical comedy stage flickered wanly in the shades of the inferno, smiling but with the fearsome rage of baffled effort. The poster bore no fulsome allusions to merits of the new food, but a single grim statement ran in bold letters along its base: "They cannot buy it now."

Spayley had grasped the fact that people will do things from a sense of duty which they would never attempt as a pleasure. There are thousands of respectable middle-class men who, if you found them unexpectedly in a sauna, would explain in all sincerity that a doctor had ordered them to take saunas. If you told them in return that you went there because you liked it, they would stare in pained wonder at the frivolity of your motive. And so it was with the new breakfast food.

No one would have eaten Filboid Studge as a pleasure, but the grim austerity of its advertisement drove parents in shoals to the grocers' shops to clamour for an immediate supply. In small kitchens, solemn pig-tailed daughters helped depressed mothers to perform the primitive ritual of its preparation. On the breakfast-tables of cheerless parlours it was partaken of in silence.

▶ Please continue to the following page

Comprehension

Once the womenfolk discovered that it was thoroughly unpalatable, their zeal in forcing it on their households knew no bounds. "You haven't eaten your Filboid Studge!" would be screamed at the appetiteless clerk as he hurried wearily from the breakfast-table, and his evening meal would be prefaced by a warmed-up mess which would be explained as "your Filboid Studge that you didn't eat this morning." Those fanatics who ostentatiously mortify themselves, inwardly and outwardly, with health biscuits and health garments, battened aggressively on the new food. A peer's daughter died from eating too much of the compound. A further advertisement was obtained when an infantry regiment mutinied when this new food was adopted as its breakfast fare.

Filboid Studge had become a household word, but its producer wisely realized that it was not necessarily the last word in breakfast diets. Its supremacy would be challenged as soon as some yet more unpalatable food should be put on the market.

Adapted from the work of H H Munro

1 Initially, what was the main advertising theme for Filboid Studge?
- **A** Eating it would make babies grow faster.
- **B** Diplomats from many countries were eager to obtain it.
- **C** Not eating Filboid Studge would tend to make you go to Hell.
- **D** It is so desirable that being unable to have it is a punishment.

2 What did the large poster depict?
- **A** People who had died were being punished for not eating their Filboid Studge.
- **B** Notable people of the day were being prevented from eating the breakfast cereal.
- **C** Authors, novelists, musicians and comedians, and others, were doing heavy work.
- **D** Famous people being forced to eat Filboid Studge.

3 How was the Filboid Studge displayed in the poster?
- **A** It was heaped upon tables at the entrance to Hell.
- **B** Depressed mothers were spooning it out to appetiteless clerks.
- **C** It was visible in see-through crockery carried by assistants of the devil.
- **D** People were eating it in saunas, either as a pleasure or as an obligation.

▶ Please continue to the following page

Comprehension

4 Which of these groups of people was specifically mentioned in the advertisement?

- **A** People whom the viewers would have recognised as having been on trial for murder
- **B** Well-known aeroplane pilots
- **C** Leaders in the business world
- **D** Television personalities noted for being able to convey emotion

5 What does the story specifically say about the poster?

- **A** It gave only sketchy details of the ingredients of the new breakfast food.
- **B** It listed names of famous people who recommended it.
- **C** It lacked any excessive praise for the breakfast food.
- **D** It showed children, plants and fungi grew more quickly after eating Filboid Studge.

6 What does the author say Spayley has understood?

- **A** Saunas are generally considered enjoyable but people don't like admitting it.
- **B** Even if asked in a serious manner, respectable middle-class men do not normally reveal that they attend saunas.
- **C** It is easier to persuade customers that they should do something, than that they would enjoy doing it.
- **D** Most users of saunas think the other attendees have come for frivolous reasons.

7 Which of the following is closest to the meaning of the word "austerity" as used by the author?

- **A** Sternness
- **B** Insistence
- **C** Luxuriance
- **D** Brevity

8 How does the author say the clerk might be affected by the new breakfast cereal?

- **A** The clerk would be given Filboid Studge as his evening meal.
- **B** Filboid Studge would be mixed into the warm course of his dinner.
- **C** The clerk would be given Filboid Studge to eat before his supper.
- **D** He would be screamed at for not having eaten Filboid Studge for breakfast and, as a punishment, not given any supper.

▶ Please continue to the following page

Comprehension

9 Which of the following is the closest in meaning to "ostentatiously"?

- A Seemingly
- B Showily
- C Secretly
- D Senselessly

10 Which of the following is the closest in meaning to "battened"?

- A Criticised
- B Coated with batter
- C Fastened
- D Deflected

11 What details were given of medical harm caused by Filboid Studge?

- A The daughter of a friend of Spayley sadly died after eating too much Filboid Studge.
- B Young girls who plaited their hair after eating it suffered a depressing level of hair loss.
- C It caused fanaticism for eating biscuits which in turn caused weight gain and ill health.
- D A lord lost a family member who was too eager with this new food.

12 How did the military become involved with Filboid Studge?

- A It became widely known that a group of soldiers refused to eat Filboid Studge
- B Spayley published an advertisement showing a regiment of infantry eating Filboid Studge in a systematic way.
- C Filboid Studge was taken on by the army and one regiment agreed to appear in a newspaper advertisement.
- D Soldiers seeing the advertisement demanded to have Filboid Studge adopted as their regiment's standard breakfast food.

13 What does the author say that Filboid Studge's producer realised?

- A A worse-tasting food might reduce the sales of Filboid Studge.
- B Filboid Studge could not always be the last part of a breakfast.
- C People would soon want to eat something else together with it at breakfast-time.
- D If a tastier food were to arrive, Filboid Studge would no longer be the top seller.

▶ Please continue to the following page

Comprehension

Below is the second passage.
Read the passage and then answer the questions that follow.
Indicate your answer by shading one of the choices A to D.

The name of the Netherlands means "Low Country", alluding to much of the country being at or below sea level, with little in the way of mountains or deep valleys. The people of the Netherlands are proud of their historical achievements, beginning in the late 16th century, of reclaiming large tracts of land from the sea and lakes. It is estimated that 17% of the country's land area was reclaimed in this way. Owing in great part to this origin, the land is fertile, permitting the Netherlands to be one of the world's largest exporters of food and dairy products. The uniquely high rate of land reclamation has come at a cost, however. The country is vulnerable to flooding, particularly if global sea levels rise, since half of the land area is either below current sea level or less than 1 metre above sea level.

On the night of 31 January 1953, a huge storm over the North Sea coincided with an unusually high tide, causing large-scale flooding in Europe, affecting the Netherlands most intensively. Almost a tenth of Dutch farmland was flooded, killing almost two thousand people and many thousand animals. In those days, none of the region's radio stations operated at night, so even though the national meteorological institute correctly predicted a large flood, the populace was oblivious.

The torrent enveloped the communication lines and extinguished the telephone and telegraph networks, propelling radio into a pivotal role for coordination. The emergency services were caught napping by the magnitude of the disaster.

With three million people living in an area on the verge of flooding, civilian volunteers rushed to shore up the crucial Schielands High Seadyke that was the only surviving bulwark against the ocean water. Despite their valiant efforts overnight, by half past five in the morning, the dyke had been definitively breached. A courageous mayor and a boat's captain together made a desperate bid to limit the consequences, ramming their vessel, the Two Brothers, into the burgeoning cavity. The crowd held their breaths.

▶ Please continue to the following page

Comprehension

14 What does the passage tell you about the landscape of the Netherlands

   A   The rugged, hilly terrain has inspired many great painters, of whom the people are proud.

   B   Deep valleys and high mountains have made the country isolated from its neighbours.

   C   The country does not have many mountains or valleys.

   D   Mountains and valleys dominate the landscape, because there is nothing to prevent it.

15 Which one of the following statements is most accurate?

   A   If sea level rises by 1 metre, half of the country will be below sea level.

   B   Half of the country is below sea level.

   C   17% of the country is below sea level

   D   The rise in sea level has caused the land to be fertile.

16 Which one of the following statements is most accurate?

   A   The Netherlands sells a great deal of food to other countries.

   B   The Netherlands profits by reclaiming land and selling it to other countries.

   C   Land reclamation from the sea is the only method of making land that costs money.

   D   The land reclamation had not started at the beginning of the year 1600.

17 Why was there so much use of radio?

   A   Telegraph operators do not work at night.

   B   Cell-phone masts were blown over by the wind, so phones could not get reception.

   C   Unlike river water, sea water is salty, and enhances phone and telegraph communication.

   D   Because of the flood, people had to use radio rather than telephone or telegraph.

18 What is stated about the emergency services?

   A   Emergency services used telephone and telegraph to evacuate the people.

   B   Because it was happening late at night, the emergency services were already asleep.

   C   The emergency services thought the flooding would be more gradual.

   D   The emergency services were not expecting a huge flood.

▶ Please continue to the following page

Comprehension

19 When the weather office predicted a large flood, how did the people of the country react?

- A They panicked, knocking holes in the thin-walled dykes, making the situation worse.
- B They ran to the beach at Schielands High Seadyke to watch the disaster unfold.
- C They did not react because they did not know about the prediction.
- D Because they thought it was caused by a meteor strike, they moved quickly.

20 How extensive was the impact of the flooding?

- A Three million people's homes were flooded.
- B One more collapsed dyke would have caused the homes of three million people to flood.
- C The flooding moved the seashore inland, to the doorsteps of three million homes.
- D Almost three million people were killed by the flood.

21 What did the people do at the Schielands High Seadyke?

- A Fear of death prevented them making efforts in the night.
- B They tried bravely to reinforce the wall.
- C They tried not to breathe in because of the unpleasant smell caused by the flood.
- D Unfortunately they had not focused on the most important problem.

22 What did the mayor and the captain do?

- A They accidentally smashed into the dyke and made a hole.
- B They tried to seal a gap in the wall.
- C They held back the crowd to protect them from the fumes.
- D Their two ships accidentally collided.

23 The passage hints that something has changed since 1953. Which of the following is it?

- A The people are more demanding of good preparation by emergency services.
- B The general population is now less brave, and less likely to help in the way described.
- C Some radio stations in the Netherlands now broadcast around the clock.
- D Boat captains and politicians in the modern day are now more likely to be enemies.

This is the end of this section. If time remains, check your answers in this section only.

Numerical Reasoning Part A

Numerical Reasoning Part A

In each of the questions, shade the correct answer option on your answer sheet.

You have 5 minutes to answer the questions in this section.

1

Every day for two weeks, Kelly adds 15 building bricks to her model house. How many bricks did she add in total?

A	B	C	D	E
30	190	210	280	290

2

Roger manages a 400 m lap of the stadium in 2 minutes. What is his average speed in km per hour?

A	B	C	D	E
8 km/hour	12 km/hour	18 km/hour	20 km/hour	200 km/hour

Note: 1 km = 1000 m 1 kilometre = 1000 metres

3

Of all 55 cars that passed the speed camera, 60% were speeding. Of the remainder, half were dirty. How many cars were neither speeding nor dirty?

A	B	C	D	E
11	15	22	25	33

4

To my already-bulging shopping bag weighing 5.4 kg, I add two cans of tuna that weigh 450 grams each. What does the bag now weigh?

A	B	C	D	E
5.9 kg	6.1 kg	6.3 kg	6.9 kg	9.9 kg

Note: 1 km = 1000 m 1 kilometre = 1000 metres

▶ Please continue to the following page

Numerical Reasoning Part A

5

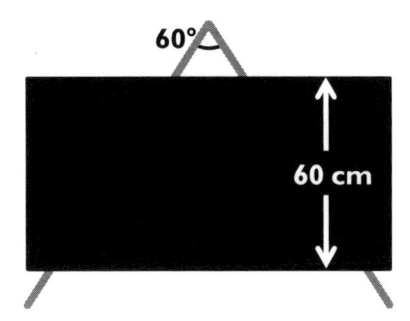

This children's blackboard has a stand (shown in grey) behind it. The feet of the stand are exactly as wide apart as the width of the blackboard itself.

The stand is symmetrical and made of two 120 cm long wooden struts.

What is the area of the blackboard?

A	B	C	D	E
120 cm²	180 cm²	240 cm²	3600 cm²	7200 cm²

6

Nelson is filling a 20 litre tank using a 2200 ml water jug, each time having to walk to the well to fill the jug first. At the outset, the jug and the tank are empty. How many trips will he need to make to fill the tank?

A	B	C	D	E
7	8	9	10	11

Note:
1 l = 1000 ml   1 litre = 1000 millilitres

A car leaves St Andrews just before lunchtime at 11:13 and arrives, 77 km away at Edinburgh Airport, at 12:08.

7 What was its average speed?

A	B	C	D	E
77 km/h	78 km/h	80 km/h	84 km/h	88 km/h

8 If it had set out at the same time but only travelled at 44 km/h, at what time would it have arrived? Give the answer in the 12-hour clock.

A	B	C	D	E
12:58 pm	1:13 pm	1:13 am	12:58 am	1:08 pm

This is the end of this section. If time remains, check your answers in this section only.

Non-Verbal Reasoning

Non-Verbal Reasoning

In each group of pictures on the left, two are missing, shown by question marks.

For each question mark, choose the picture on the right that is best suited to be the missing picture. Shade your answer on the answer sheet by choosing from the options A to F.

You have 7 minutes to answer the questions in this section.

1, 2

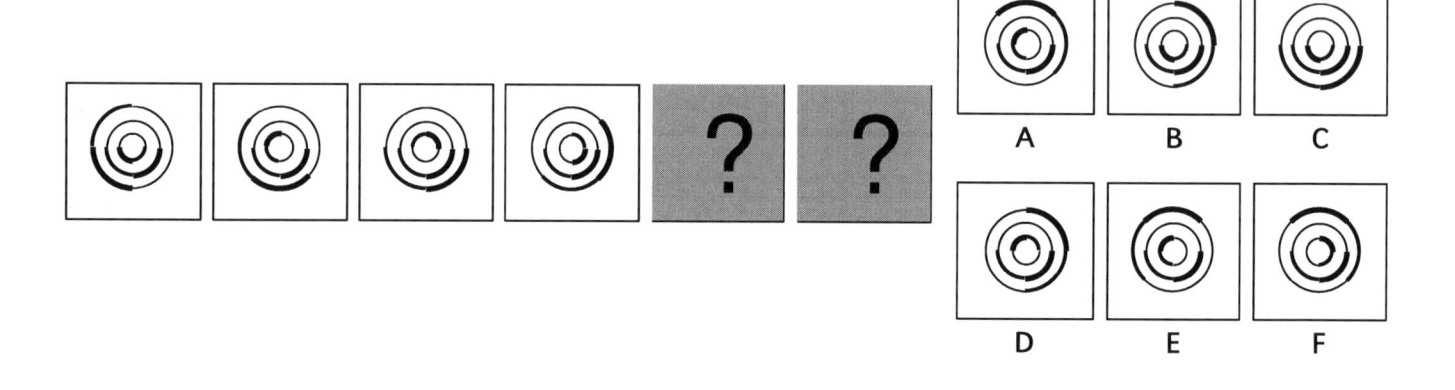

3, 4

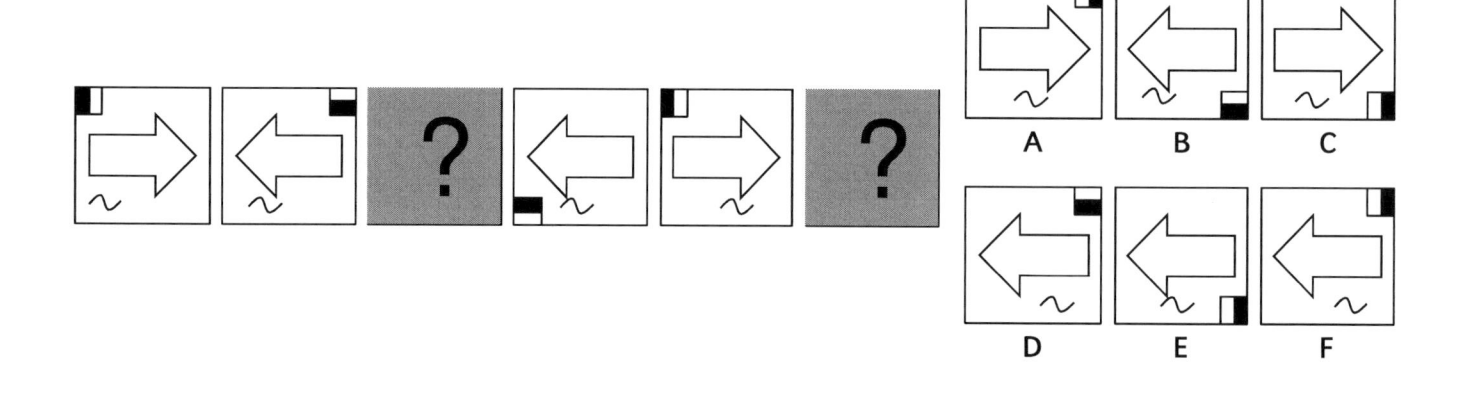

▶ Please continue to the following page

Non-Verbal Reasoning

5, 6

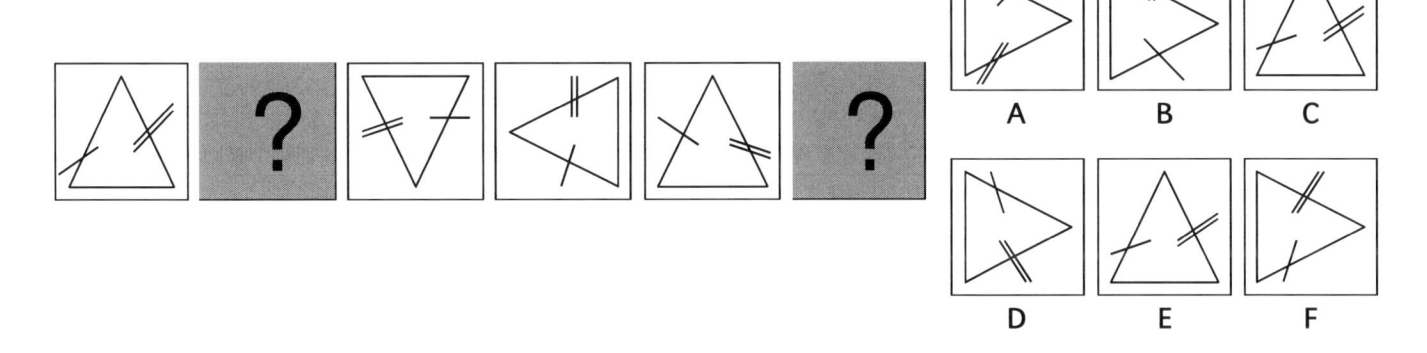

7, 8

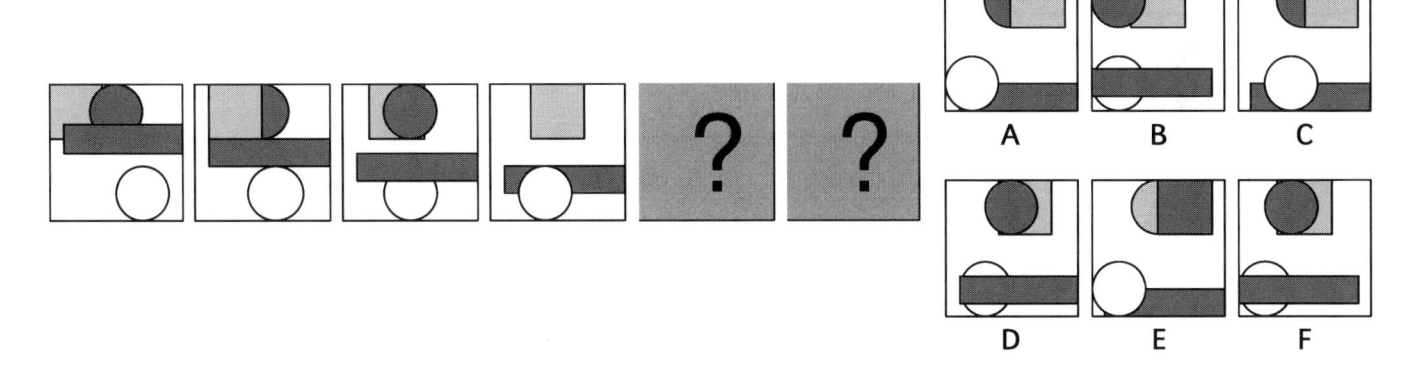

9, 10

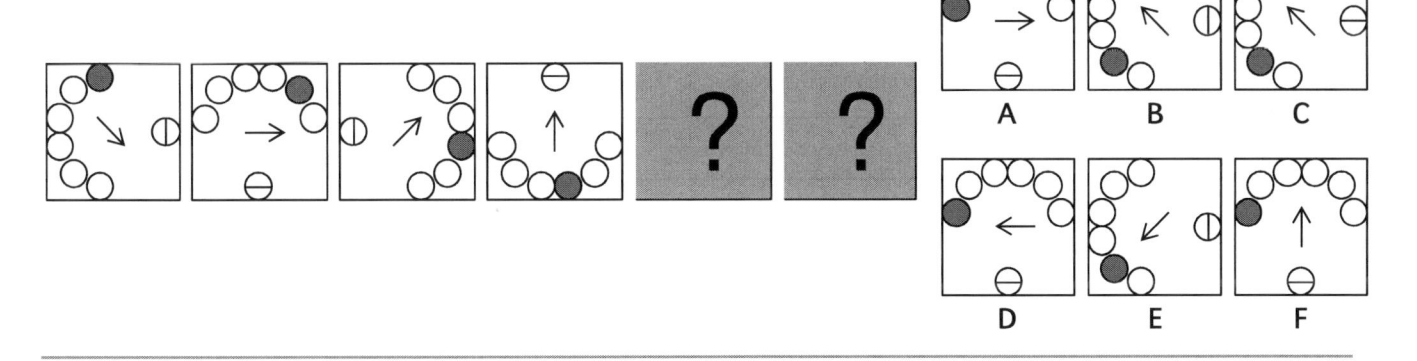

▶ Please continue to the following page

Non-Verbal Reasoning

11, 12

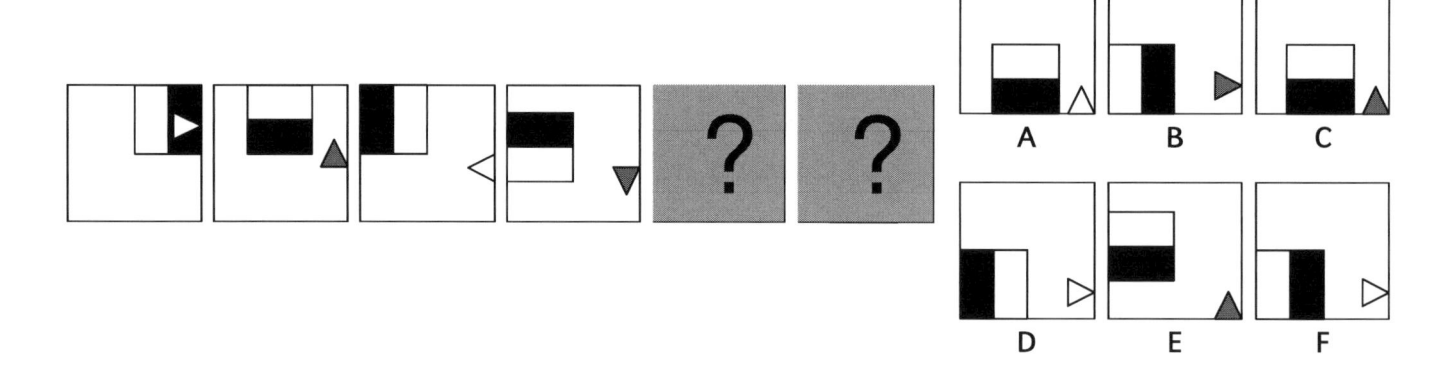

13, 14

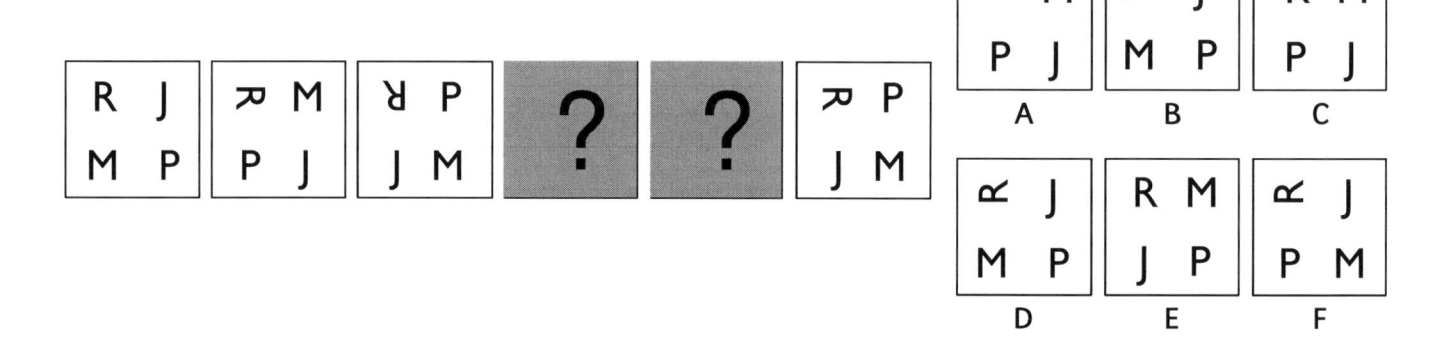

15, 16

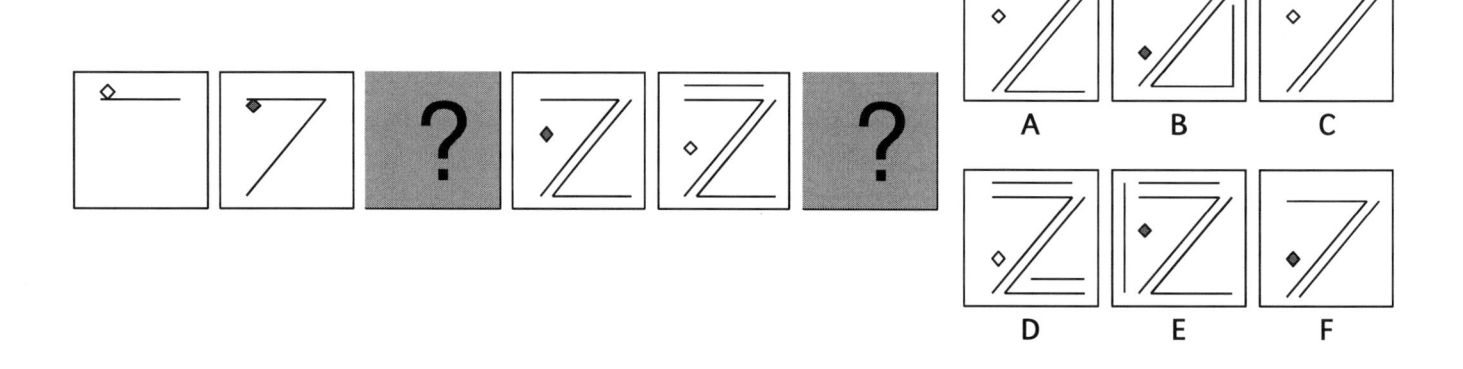

This is the end of this section. If time remains, check your answers in this section only.

Numerical Reasoning Part B

Numerical Reasoning Part B

Write the two digits, one in each box. Put a zero in the first box if your answer is less than 10. Shade one box in each column, corresponding to the digits.

You have 5 minutes to answer the questions in this section.

1

Our school's 72,000 litre swimming pool is only a quarter full this morning. If we pour in water at 1 litre per second, how many hours will it take to become full?

2

Sock colour	Number
Red	4
Blue	12
Black	24
White	8
Green	2

At my school prize-giving ceremony I am only allowed to wear white or black socks, although I have socks of many colours, as shown in this table.

What percentage of my socks are white or black?

3

Pippa is planning to pave a 1.5 metre wide, 9 metre long path in her garden. In the shop, she has found beige square paving tiles that measure 50 cm on each side. How many does she need?

Note:
1m = 100 cm   1 metre = 100 centimetres

4

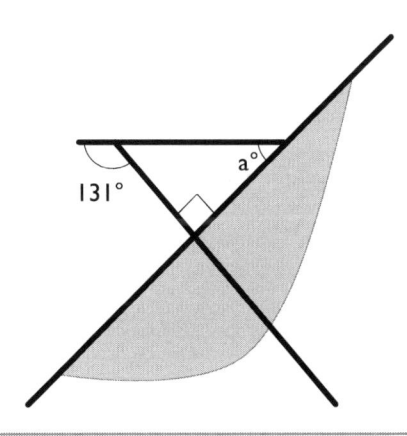

In this side view sketch of a deckchair, how many degrees is the angle marked a°?

▶ Please continue to the following page

Numerical Reasoning Part B

Suppose a new mathematical symbol, ❖, is introduced. It is placed between two values, and is defined to mean add the two values together and then square the result.

For example, $3 ❖ 4 = (3+4)^2 = 7^2 = 49$.

5

What is $6 ❖ 3$?

6

If $q ❖ 7 = 400$, and you know q is a positive whole number, what is q?

7

The Royal Mint reports that 3% of all pound coins in circulation are counterfeit. The pound coins collected at the school fete totalled £250 in the morning and a separate £350 in the afternoon. How many counterfeit pound coins should be expected amongst the total collection of the day?

8

The beautifully symmetrical lawn sketched here fits within a square garden, but has curved "bites" taken out of each side for flower beds.

What is the perimeter of the lawn?

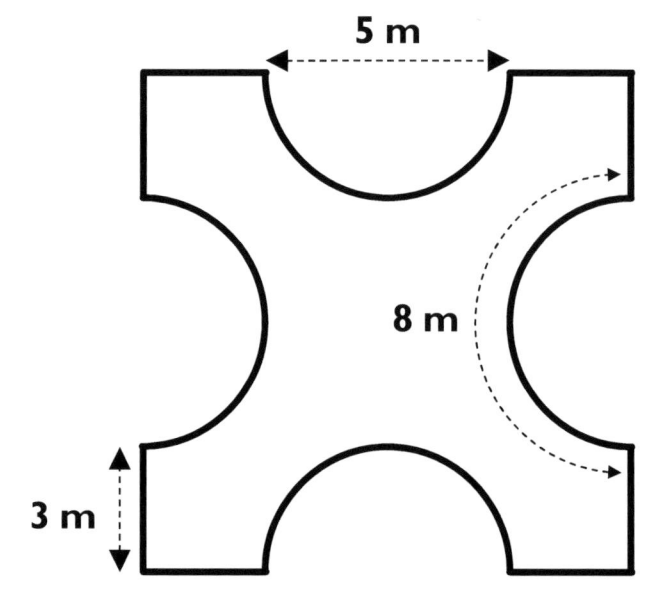

This is the end of the test. If time remains, check your answers in this section only.

Paper G

Numerical Reasoning

On each page there are questions whose answers are numbers, given in the table at the top of the page.

For each question, choose the letter A to J which represents the correct answer. Mark your answer on the answer sheet.

You have 12 minutes to answer the questions in this section.

A	B	C	D	E	F	G	H	I	J
1/2	1/4	3/5	2/3	9/20	1 1/2	1 1/5	1/36	1/60	1/100

1 Roxanne has a long toy storage unit at the foot of her bed. The unit is 2 metres wide, 50 cm tall and 60 cm from front to back. What is its volume in m^3?

2 Currently she only has in it one box that is 20 cm × 15 cm × 20 cm. What fraction of the toy storage unit is occupied?

3 She decides to paint the top of the storage unit. How many m^2 is its area?

Clifford throws two standard six-sided dice, one white and one black.

4 What is the probability that the white die scores an even number?

5 What is the chance that the black die scores more than 2?

6 What is the probability his total score, from the two dice, is 2?

---

7 "The remainder of our 50 animals are cats," concluded Doris after listing the 5 collie dogs, 8 labrador dogs, and 7 retriever dogs. What proportion of the dogs are collies?

8 What proportion of the animals are cats?

9 If 10 cats were moved to another sanctuary, what proportion of the remaining animals would be dogs?

▶ Please continue to the following page

Numerical Reasoning

A	B	C	D	E	F	G	H	I	J
1	2	4	20	36	40	120	132	400	2250

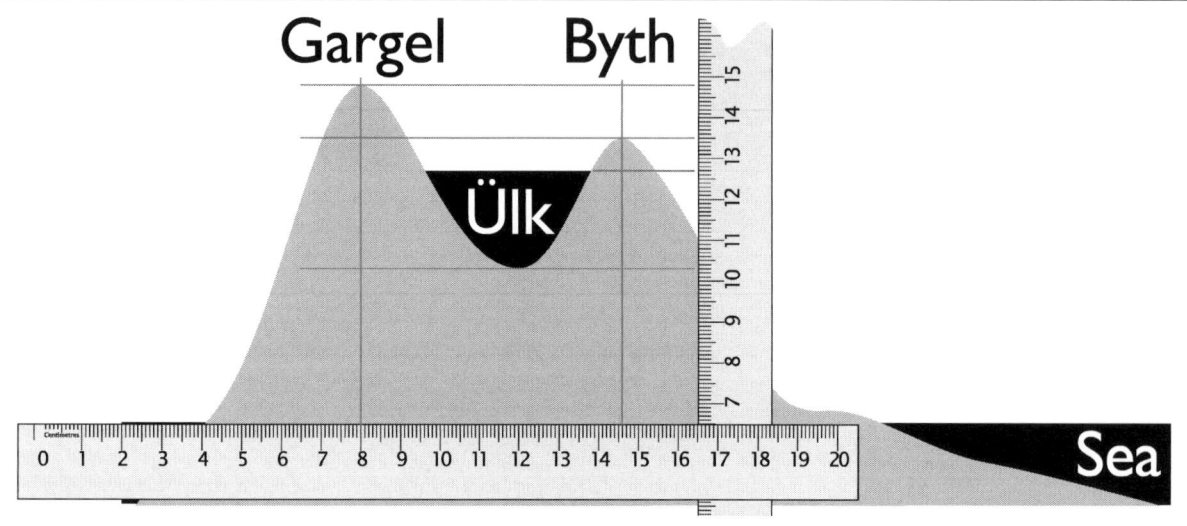

Two hills, Gargel and Byth, have lake Ülk between them. On this sketch, horizontal distance is on a 1 : 2 000 000 scale. Altitude is on a 1:5000 scale. Two rulers marked in centimetres are also shown.

Note:
1 m = 100 cm.   1 metre = 100 centimetres.   1 km = 1000 m.   1 kilometre = 1000 metres.

10 How many kilometres is the horizontal distance between the tops of Gargel and Byth?

11 How deep is lake Ülk, in metres?

12 If something is square on the sketch, how many times wider is it than tall, in real life?

Fatima moves to a car sales job paying £ 15 000 per year plus £ 500 per car she sells.

13 If she sells 2 cars a month, how many pounds (£) will her monthly pay be?

14 She actually earns £ 35 000 in her first year. How many cars did she sell that year?

15 What percentage increase is this over her previous year's earnings of £ 25 000?

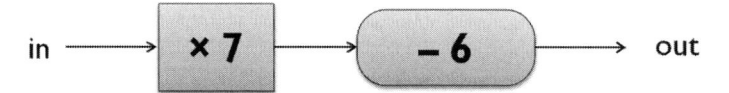

---

in → ×7 → −6 → out

16 If 6 is fed in to the machine above, what result does it produce?

17 With a different input, the machine produces a result 134. What number was put in?

18 Which number, if fed in, comes out identical as the output?

This is the end of this section. If time remains, check your answers in this section only.

Non-verbal Reasoning

Paper **G** Page **3**

Non-verbal Reasoning

In the following questions, on the left is the net of a cube.

Choose the picture of a cube on the right that is best suited to the net. Shade your answer on the answer sheet by choosing one of the options A to F.

You have 12 minutes to answer the questions in this section.

Example

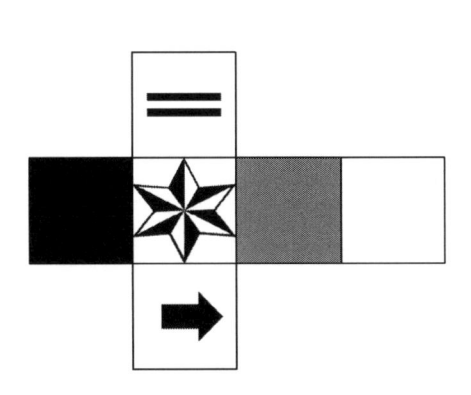

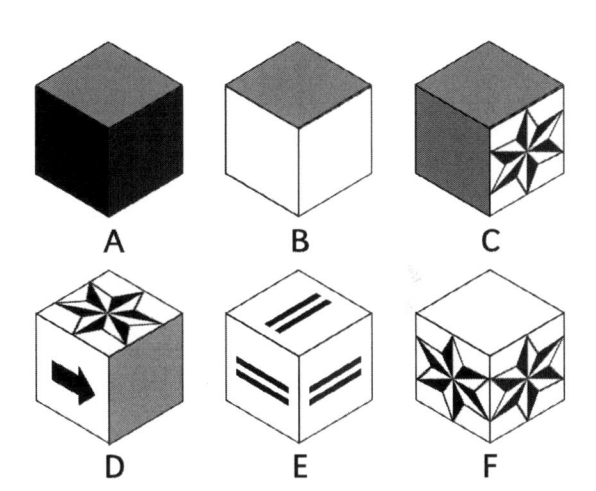

The correct answer is D. Mark it as shown below.

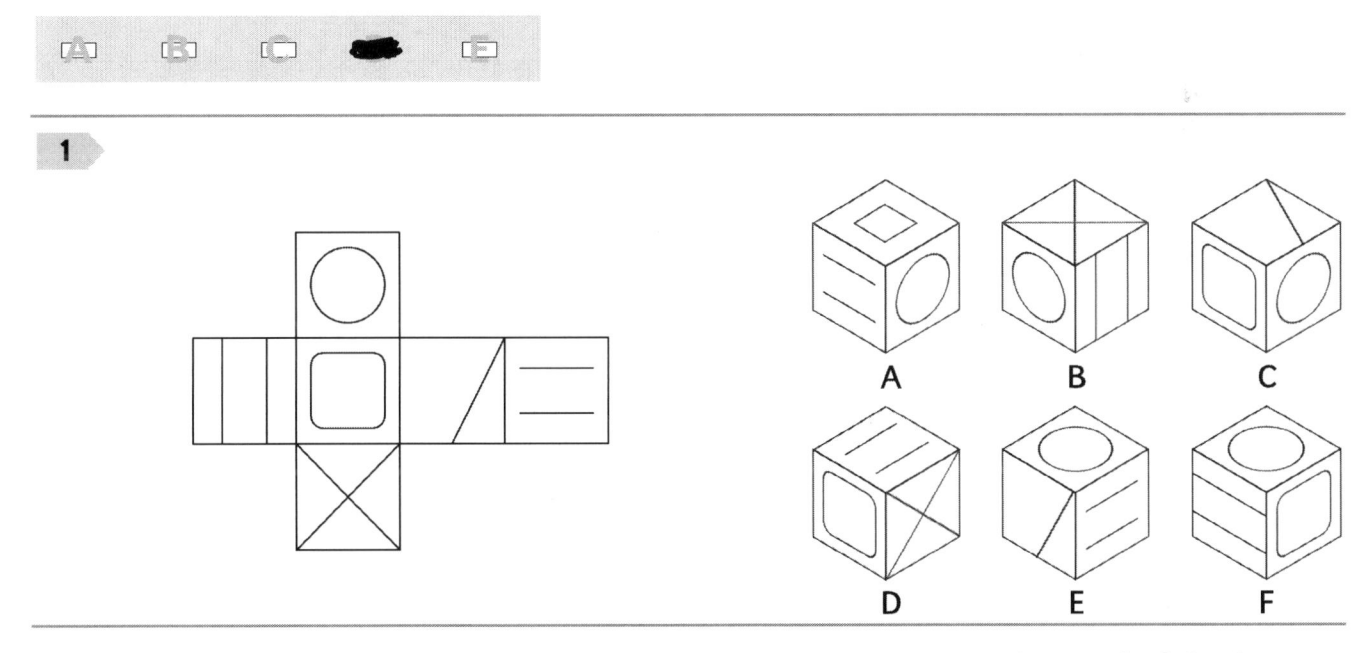

1

▶ Please continue to the following page

Non-verbal Reasoning

Paper **G** Page **4**

2

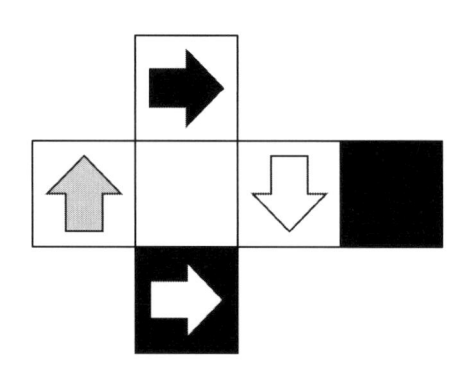

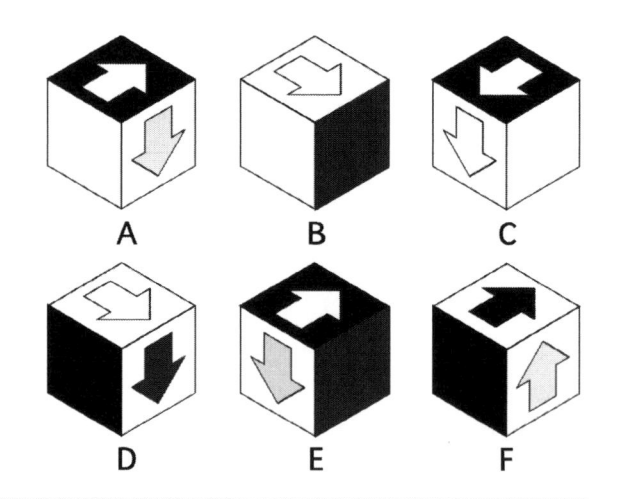

3

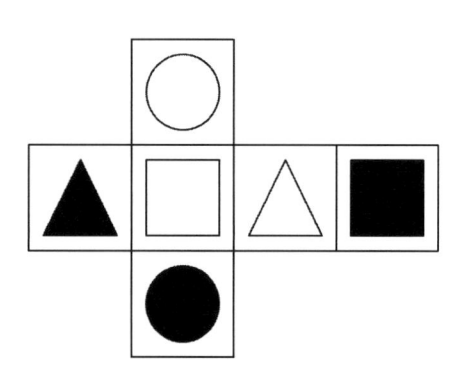

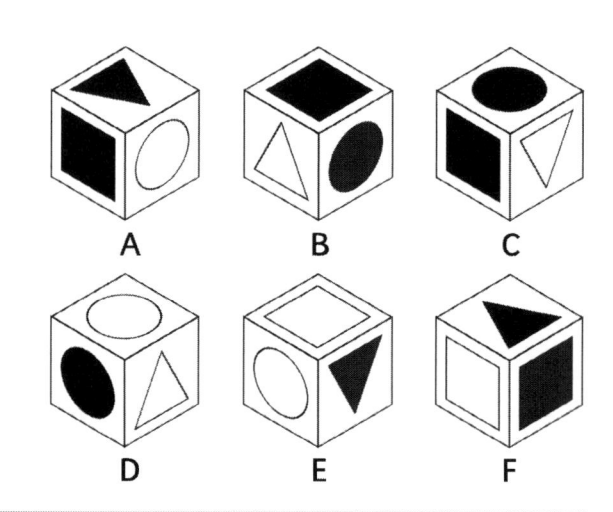

4

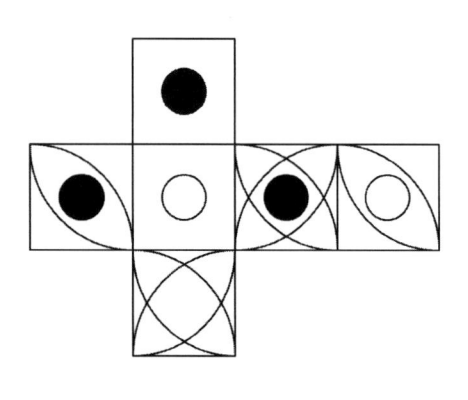

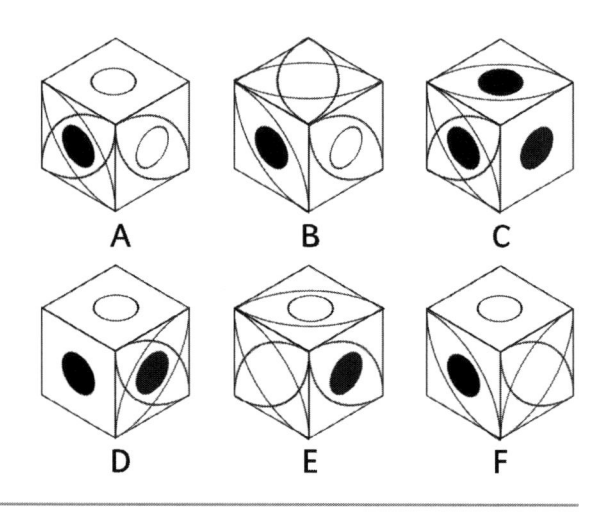

▶ Please continue to the following page

Non-verbal Reasoning

5

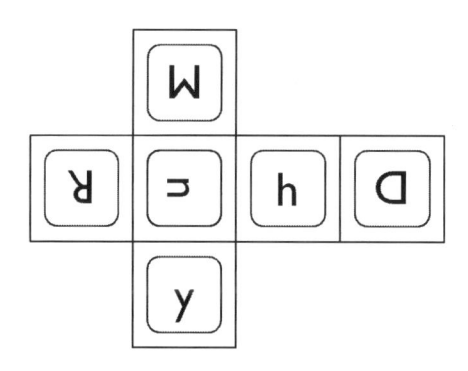

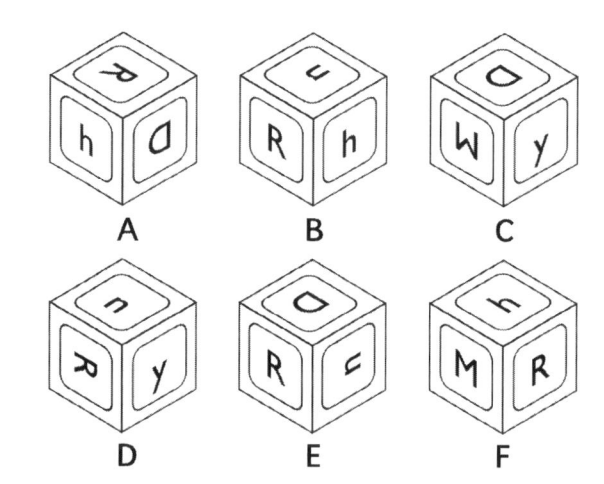

6

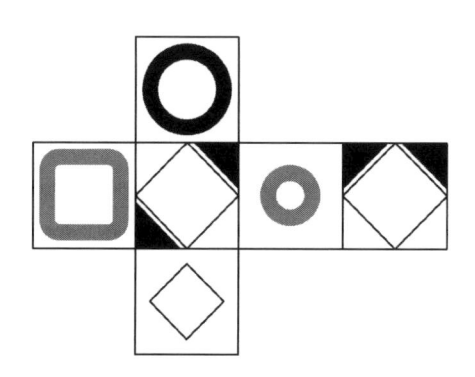

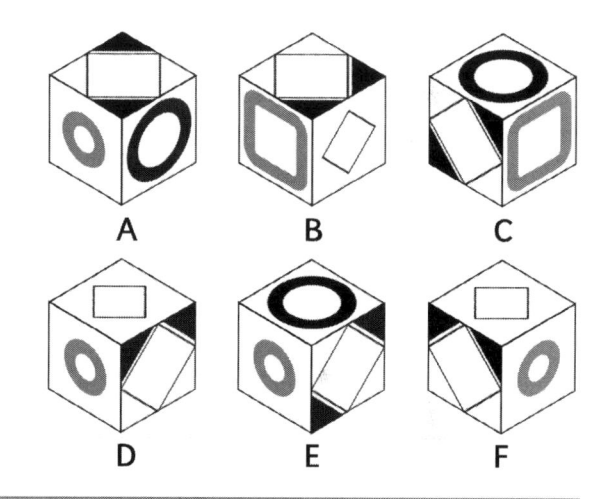

7

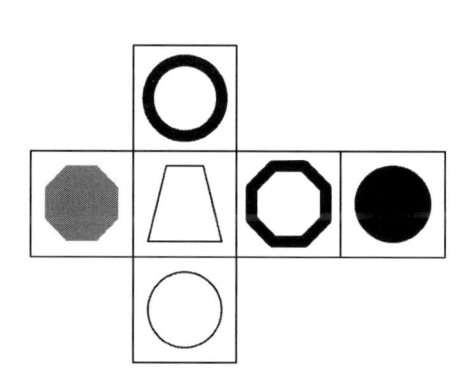

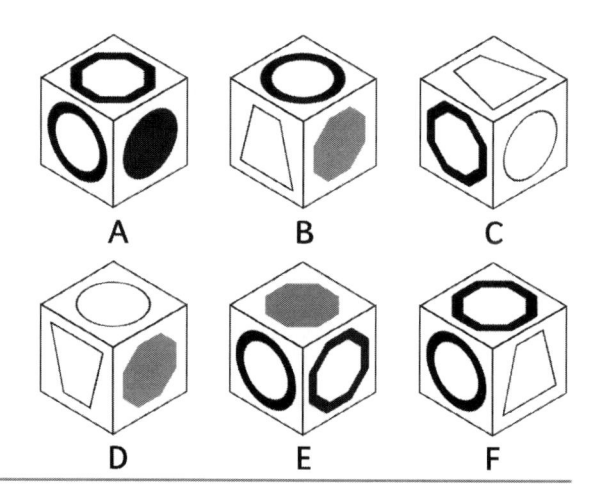

▶ Please continue to the following page

Non-verbal Reasoning

Paper **G** Page **6**

8

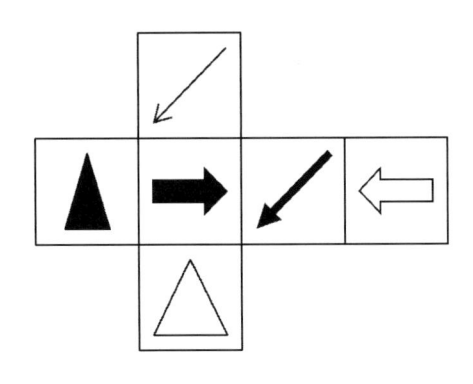

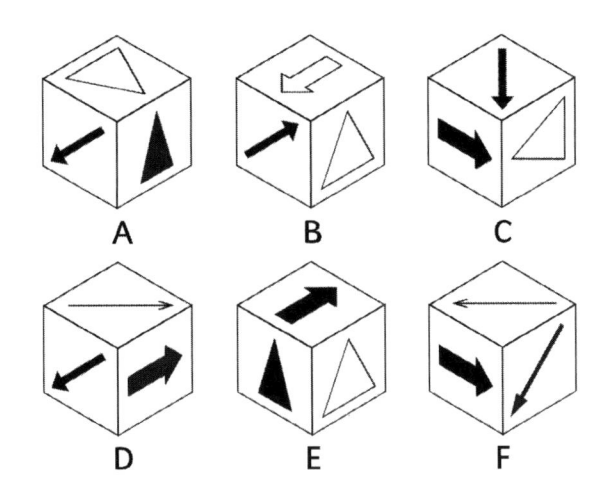

9

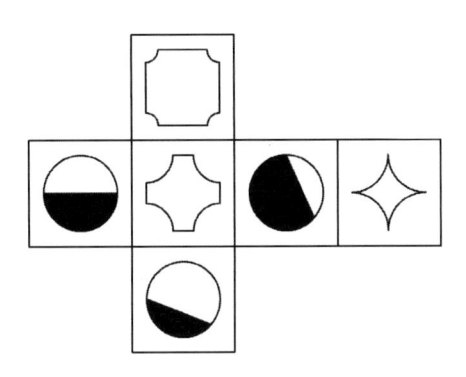

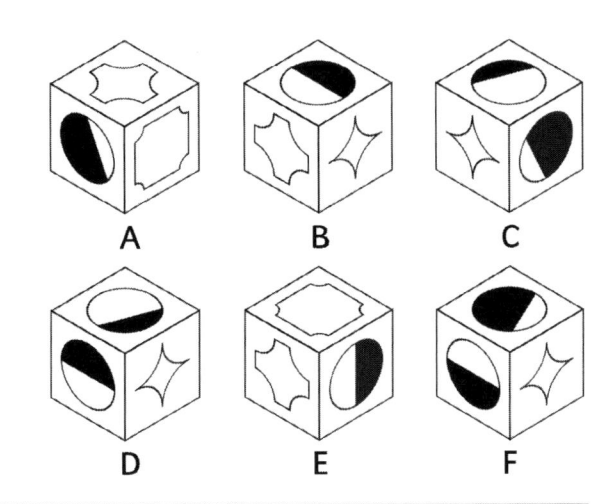

10

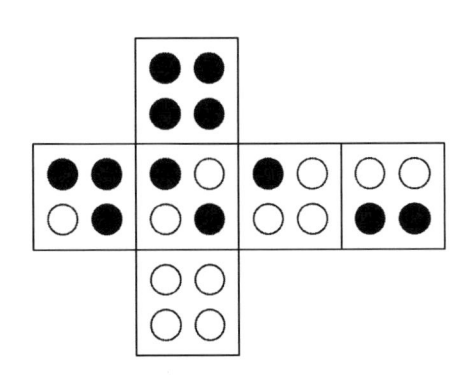

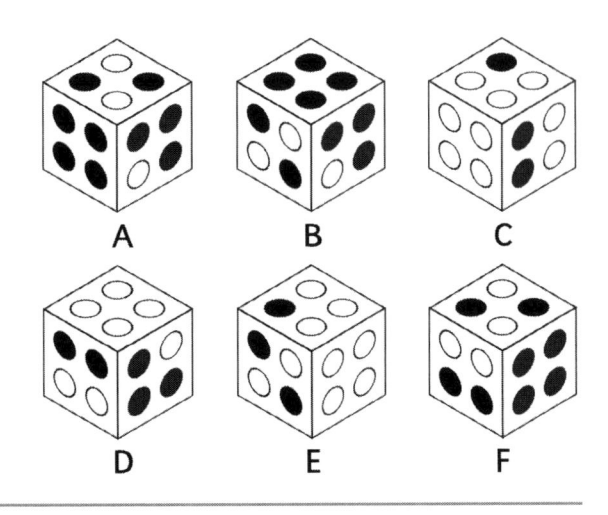

▶ Please continue to the following page

Non-verbal Reasoning

Paper **G** Page **7**

11

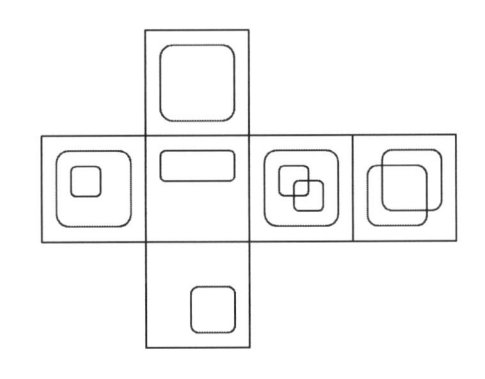

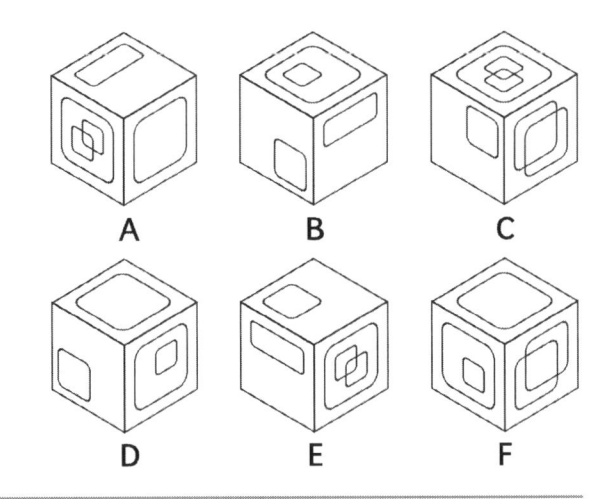

A   B   C
D   E   F

12

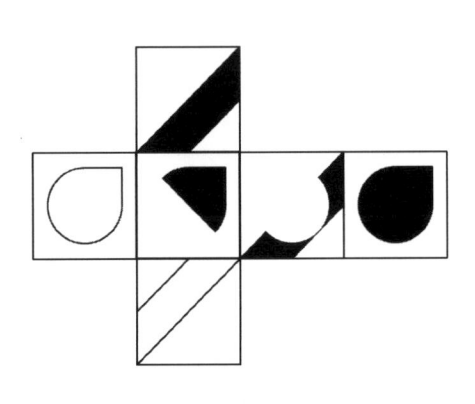

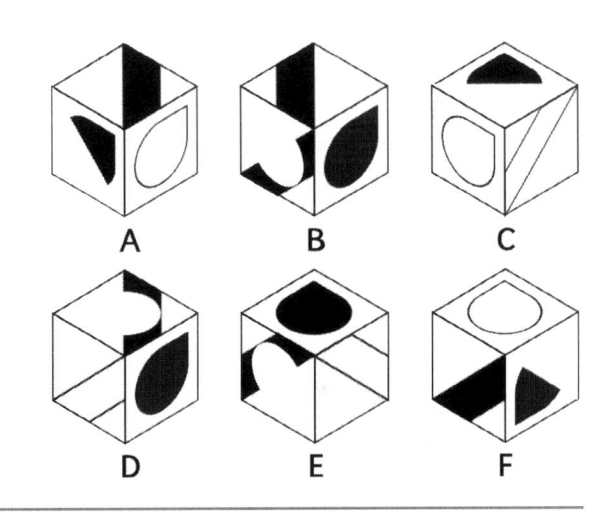

A   B   C
D   E   F

13

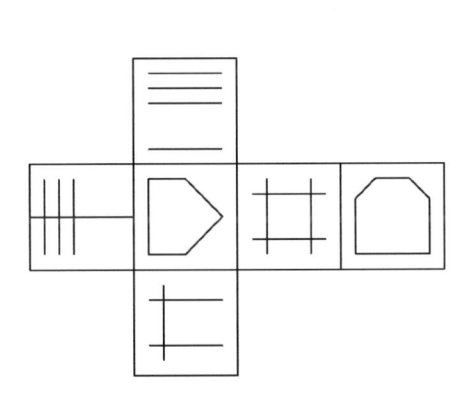

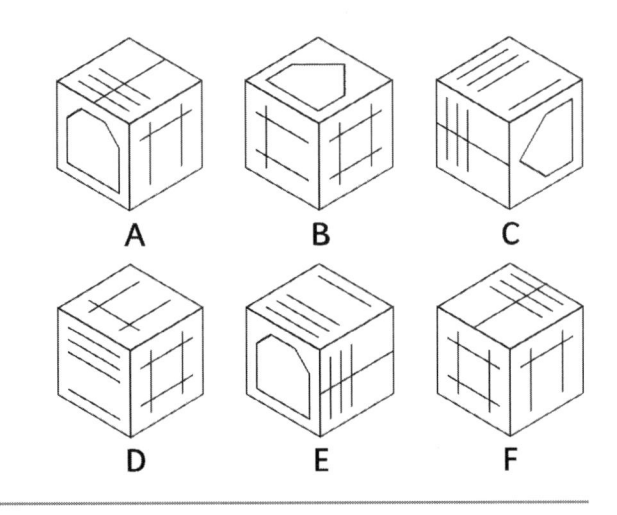

A   B   C
D   E   F

❌ **This is the end of this section. If time remains, check your answers in this section only.**

Find the Missing Words

Find the Missing Words

In the passage below, at several positions several options are shown for a missing word. In each case choose the word that fits best, and shade your answer A-E on the answer sheet.

You have 10 minutes to answer the questions in this section.

Curiously worded right from its title, Ring a Ring o' Roses is a classic children's nursery **1**
A class
B test
C rhyme
D school
E law

that has been a favourite for over a **2**
A mountain
B lunchtime
C break
D many
E century
, with few giving thought to the origin of the odd

3
A language
B numbers
C people
D words
E sight
that does not have an obvious meaning in **4**
A occasional
B everyday
C spoken
D nocturnal
E library
life. Those who

5
A don't
B prevent
C tread
D dissuade
E probe
a little may find that phrases in the song are said to **6**
A represent
B delivering
C direct
D corresponding
E return
aspects of

the Black Death, a great plague that **7**
A enlivened
B destroy
C created
D devastated
E decimate
much of England in the late 1600s, wiping out

large

▶ Please continue to the following page

Find the Missing Words

swathes of the **8**
- A population
- B decade
- C flora
- D livestock
- E fauna

of the country and rendering some smaller settlements into virtual

9
- A commuter
- B larger
- C ghost
- D electronic
- E computer

towns. The symptoms of this terrible disease are said to **10**
- A include
- B awful
- C terrible
- D having
- E comprising

pink coloration of the cheeks, explaining the "ring of roses", and sometimes **11**
- A circles
- B thorns
- C sneezing
- D guesswork
- E paper-thin

, presumed the origin of the phrase "atishoo, atishoo". Most people who **12**
- A contracted
- B enlarged
- C improved
- D shrunken
- E recovered

the plague would not survive a week. During this time they would be **13**
- A quarantined
- B unharmed
- C colluding
- D infectious
- E hospitalised

, putting the lives of their nearest and dearest at risk. Some people of the time believed that herbs, carried in bunches (or "posies") could

14
- A help
- B ward
- C attract
- D smell
- E protect

off the evil disease, explaining the term "pocketful of posies". **15**
- A Therefore
- B However,
- C Consequently, we
- D Immediately,
- E Unnecessarily

▶ Please continue to the following page

Find the Missing Words

should not assume that this logical-sounding explanation is correct. **16**
- A Beside
- B After
- C Since
- D Before
- E Along

1940, despite

many scholars speculating on the origin of the song, none mentioned a **17**
- A link
- B tune
- C plague
- D likely
- E association

to the

Black Death. For unclear reasons, by about 1950, the Black Death explanation had appeared and

become **18**
- A main
- B largest
- C preferring
- D fatal
- E dominant

. How this happened we may **19**
- A tremble
- B speculate
- C never
- D fear
- E theorise

learn, but it is difficult to

understand how accurate information about **20**
- A tens
- B events
- C person
- D thousands
- E pestilential

of hundreds of years ago could have

suddenly **21**
- A emerged
- B came
- C remembered
- D disappeared
- E surface

and been incorporated into modern scholarship without anyone

recording **22**
- A with
- B machine
- C as
- D how
- E sound

this new knowledge came to light. It is therefore entirely **23**
- A certain
- B possible
- C clear
- D unlikely
- E definite

that the explanation was simply made up in the mid 1900s. Its plausibility might have contributed to the ease with which the story spread.

❌ **This is the end of this section. If time remains, check your answers in this section only.**

Groups

In each question, one of the words on the right is a member of the group shown on the left.

Choose the single most suitable group member from options A to E. Shade your one chosen answer on the answer sheet.

You have 11 minutes to answer the questions in this section.

1 luggage

A	B	C	D	E
receiver	rucksack	trolley	barrel	conveyer

2 material

A	B	C	D	E
solid	viable	director	lead	dress

3 modification

A	B	C	D	E
truncation	presentation	insinuation	calculation	repetition

4 amphibian

A	B	C	D	E
whale	donkey	kangaroo	hornet	frog

5 pointer

A	B	C	D	E
arrow	position	pathway	choice	noticeboard

6 equipment

A	B	C	D	E
remorse	assets	concept	console	preparation

7 image

A	B	C	D	E
insight	reflection	thought	speculate	reputation

8 athlete

A	B	C	D	E
sprint	runner	carpet	javelin	spectator

▶ Please continue to the following page

Groups

		A	B	C	D	E
9	brown	khaki	boulder	bear	granite	aquamarine

		A	B	C	D	E
10	segment	feature	television	slice	following	increase

		A	B	C	D	E
11	costume	fancy	leotard	outfit	fragrance	flexible

		A	B	C	D	E
12	season	salty	spiced	wintry	spring	autumnal

		A	B	C	D	E
13	gap	chasm	gradation	option	steering	gantry

		A	B	C	D	E
14	rivers	swirls	rapids	overturn	complexes	velocities

		A	B	C	D	E
15	indicate	align	pathway	jostle	pixel	point

		A	B	C	D	E
16	quantity	due	lute	lug	glut	glue

		A	B	C	D	E
17	statement	conclusion	bank	bulwark	philosophy	signal

		A	B	C	D	E
18	reshape	mould	liberate	scale	restart	monkey

▶ Please continue to the following page

Groups

		A	B	C	D	E
19	capital	Berlin	Manchester	Rhine	Asia	Argentina

		A	B	C	D	E
20	allocate	remove	transfer	raffle	implicate	simplify

		A	B	C	D	E
21	shape	wood	fire	water	coal	diamond

		A	B	C	D	E
22	condiment	ketchup	drums	soup	fork	backup

		A	B	C	D	E
23	ointment	paracetamol	salve	perfume	spectacles	bracket

		A	B	C	D	E
24	quadruped	snake	eagle	human	cat	centipede

		A	B	C	D	E
25	ancestor	grandmother	niece	daughter	son	sister

		A	B	C	D	E
26	irritation	anger	depression	itch	anxiety	lotion

		A	B	C	D	E
27	organ	salamander	chestnut	pipe	engine	liver

		A	B	C	D	E
28	stone	mountain	amethyst	grinding	glass	weight

This is the end of the test. If time remains, check your answers in this section only.

Paper H

Shuffled Sentences

Each sentence has had its words shuffled and an additional word inserted. Identify the additional word. Mark the option A to E on your answer sheet.

You have 6 minutes to answer the questions in this section.

1

substitute no work is there player hard for

A	B	C	D	E
no	substitute	player	work	hard

2

cave he bright the into the sun from emerged at summer escaped last

A	B	C	D	E
into	he	escaped	from	cave

3

unhealthy anger were biscuits and cakes his foods being despite favourite

A	B	C	D	E
his	anger	being	unhealthy	favourite

▶ Please continue to the following page

Shuffled Sentences

Paper H — Page 2

4

a bread roll the the revealed of magician after grand hat the drum contents

A	B	C	D	E
roll	of	bread	the	magician

5

delayed order hamburger the was considerably begin to

A	B	C	D	E
hamburger	order	delayed	was	begin

6

while your market stall finish wrapping his brother present i

A	B	C	D	E
brother	while	your	market	stall

7

polish a silver spoon sent us a shone friend

A	B	C	D	E
spoon	polish	sent	shone	a

8

shreds a tissue well for as the reaches up he tears

A	B	C	D	E
well	shreds	for	reaches	tissue

❌ **This is the end of this section. If time remains, check your answers in this section only.**

Non-verbal Reasoning

Non-verbal Reasoning

In each group of pictures on the left, one is missing, shown by a question mark. Choose the picture on the right that is best suited to be the missing picture.

Shade your answer on the answer sheet by choosing one of the options A to F.

You have 6 minutes to answer the questions in this section.

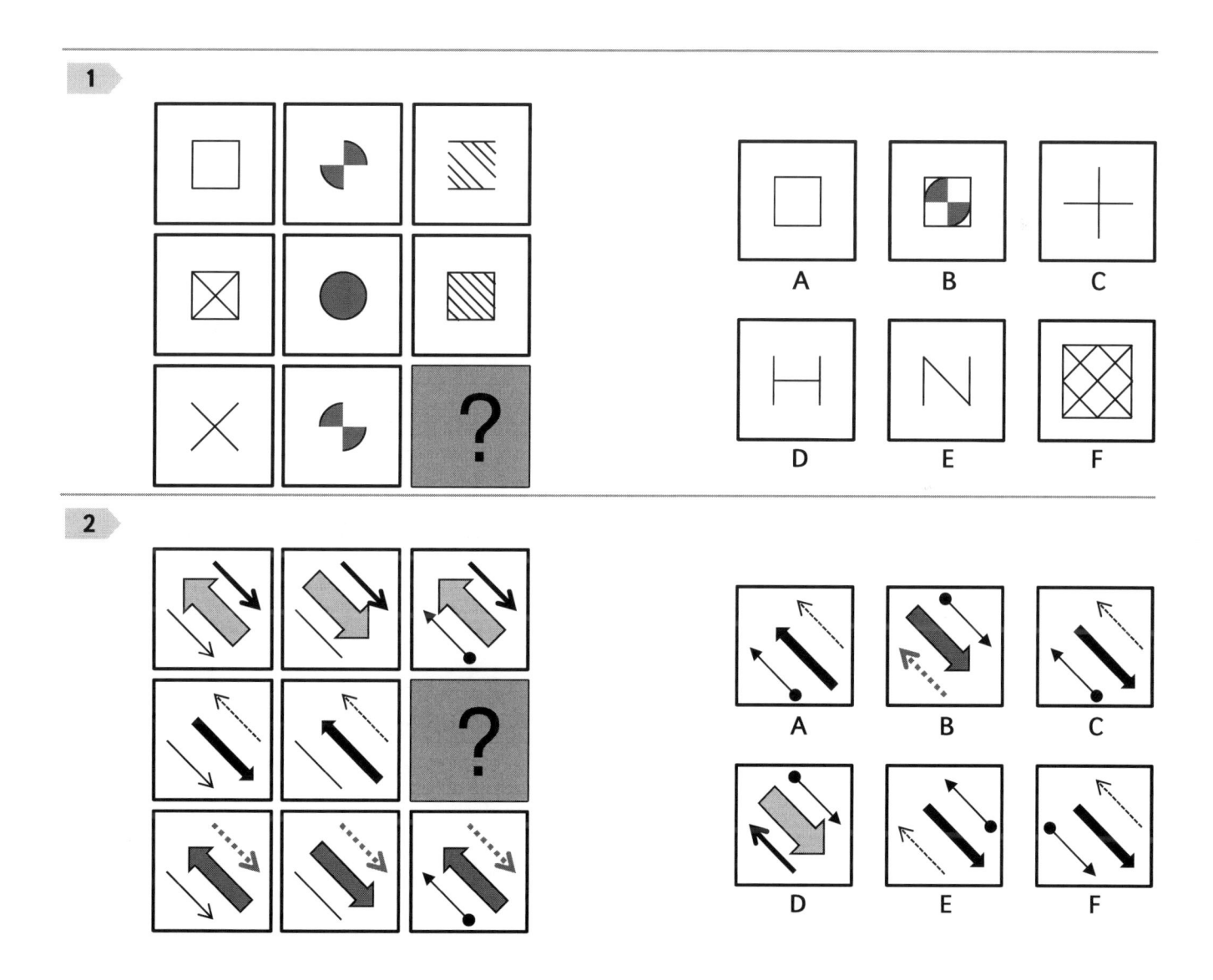

1

2

Please continue to the following page

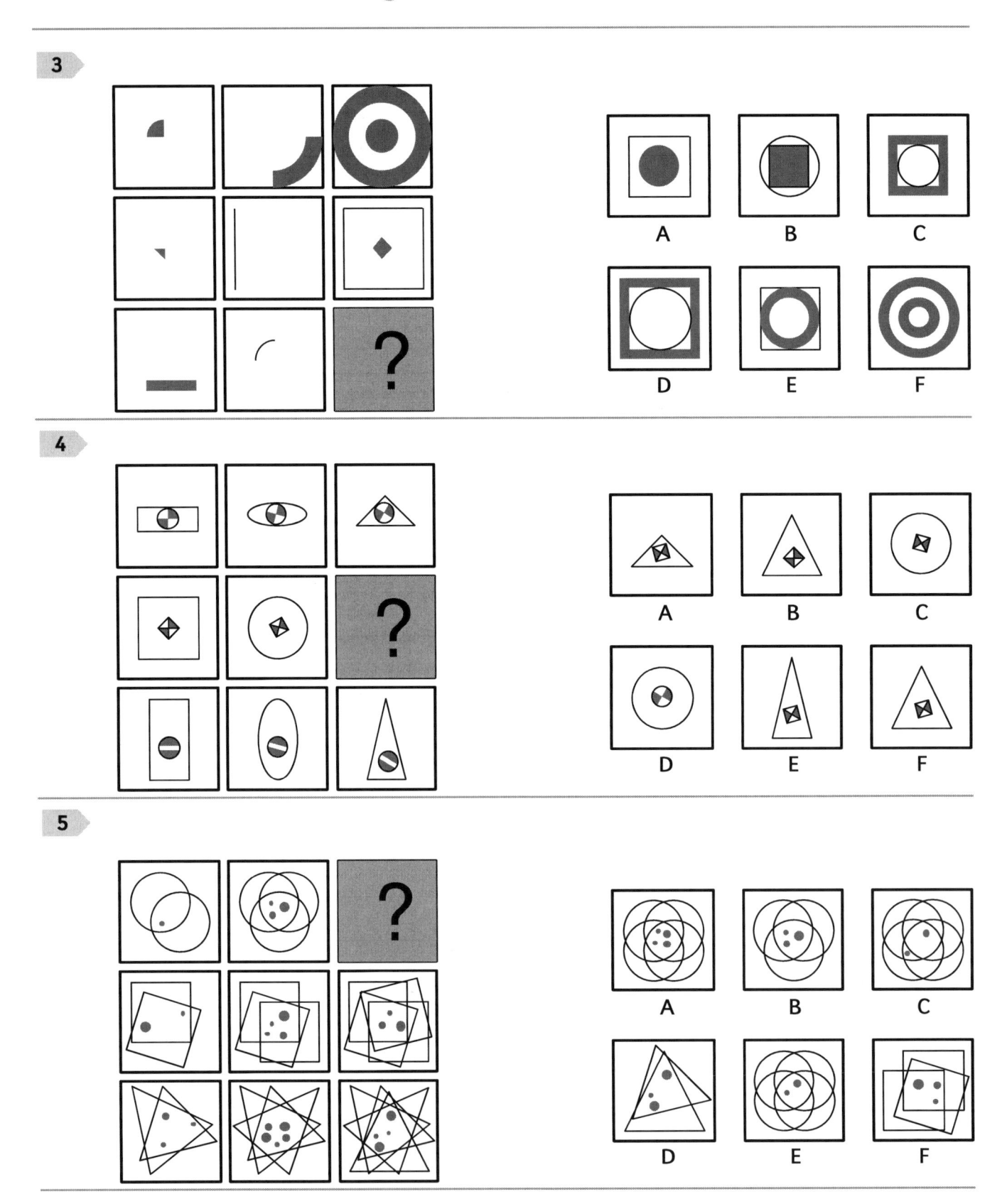

Non-verbal Reasoning

3

4

5

▶ Please continue to the following page

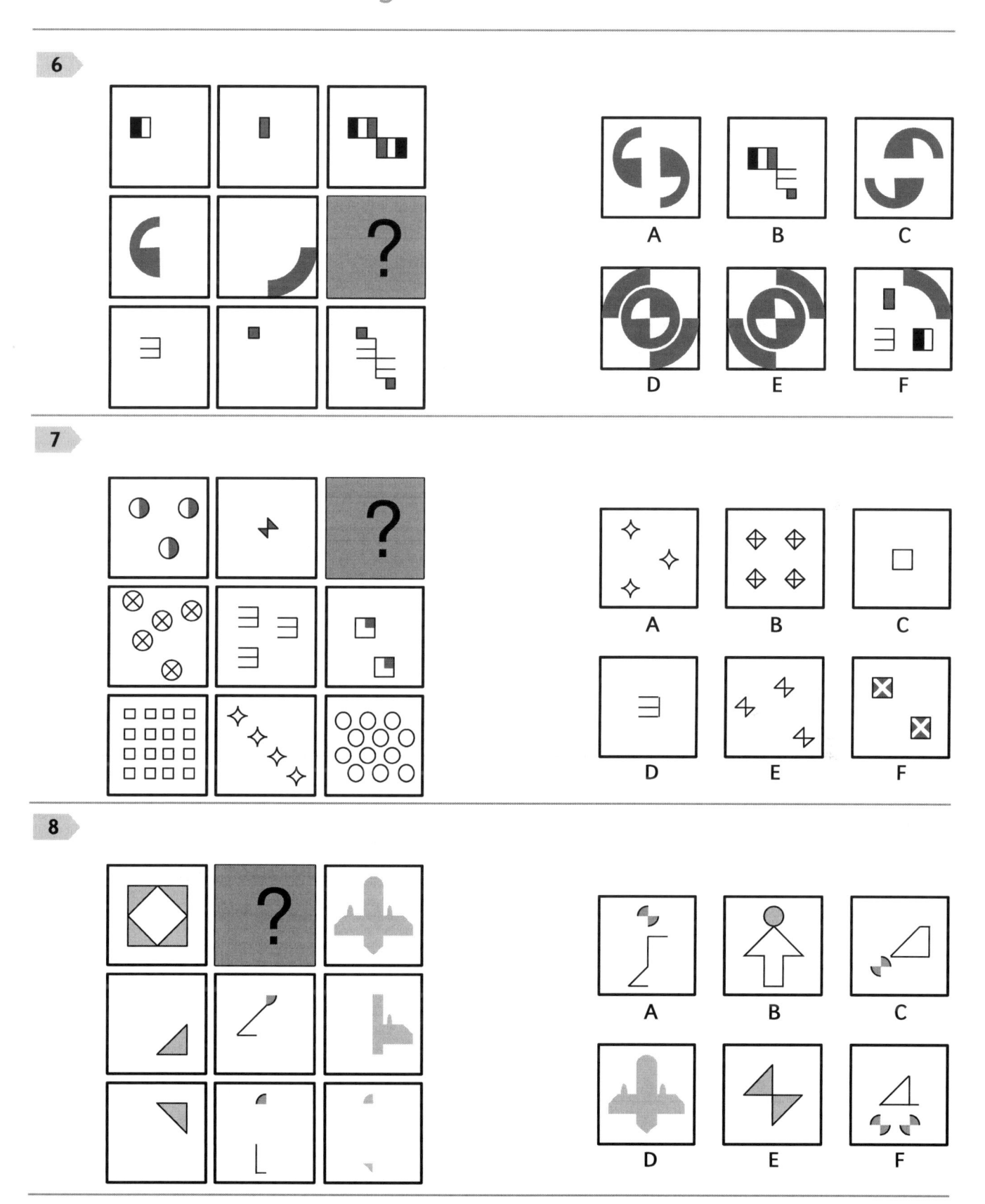

Non-verbal Reasoning

Paper H Page 5

6

7

8

▶ Please continue to the following page

Non-verbal Reasoning

Paper **H** Page 6

9

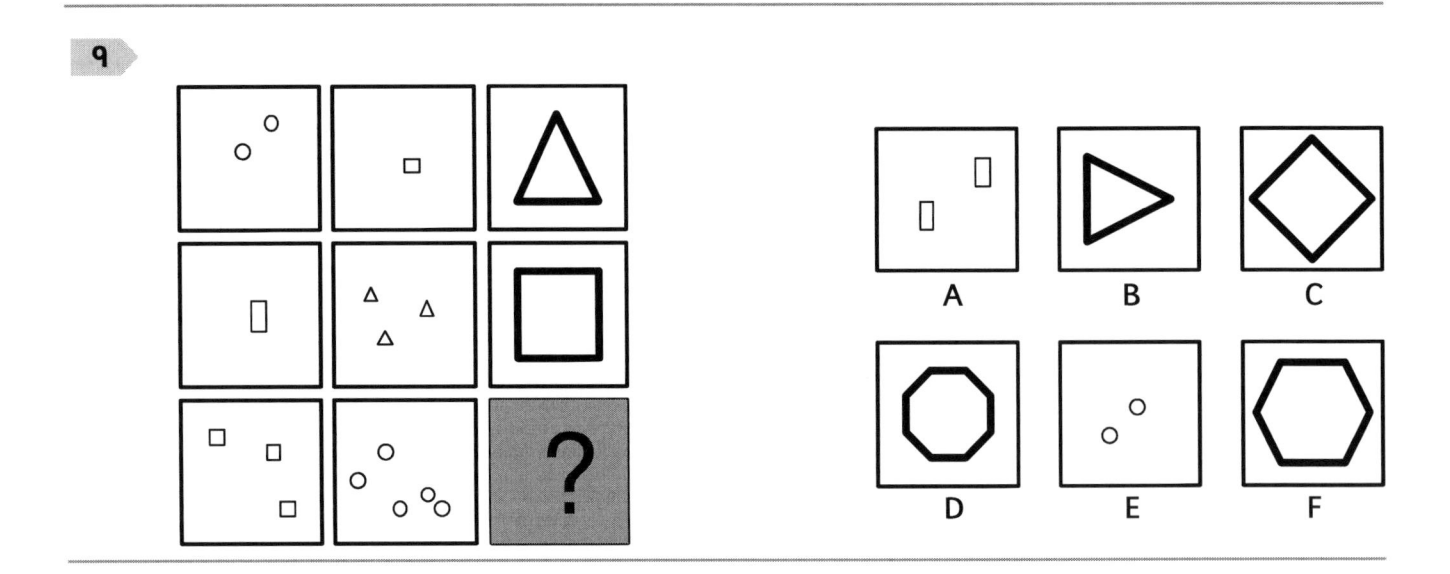

This is the end of this section. If time remains, check your answers in this section only.

Comprehension

Comprehension

Read the passage below and then answer the questions that follow.
Indicate your answer by shading one of the choices A to D.
You have **11** minutes to answer the questions in this section.

I was so pleased at having given the slip to Long John that I began to enjoy myself and look around me with some interest on the strange land that I was in. First I crossed a marshy tract full of willows, bulrushes, and outlandish, swampy trees. I came out upon the skirts of an open piece of undulating, sandy country about a mile long. Dotted with a few pines, it bore a great many contorted trees, not unlike the oak in growth, but pale in the foliage, like willows. On the far side of the open stood one of the hills, with two quaint, craggy peaks shining vividly in the sun.

I now felt for the first time the joy of exploration. The isle was uninhabited; my shipmates I had left behind, and nothing lived in front of me but dumb brutes and fowls. I turned hither and thither among the trees. Here and there were flowering plants, unknown to me. Occasionally I saw snakes, and one raised his head from a ledge of rock and hissed at me with a noise not unlike the spinning of a top. Little did I suppose that he was a deadly enemy and that the noise was the famous rattle.

Then I came to a long thicket of these oaklike trees—live, or evergreen, oaks, I heard afterwards they should be called. They grew low along the sand like brambles, the boughs curiously twisted, the foliage compact, like thatch. The thicket stretched down from one of the knolls, spreading and growing taller as it went, until it reached the margin of the broad, reedy fen. Through this the nearest of the little rivers soaked its way into the anchorage. The marsh was steaming in the strong sun, and the outline of Spyglass Hill trembled through the haze.

All at once there was a bustle among the bulrushes. A wild duck flew up with a quack, another followed, and soon over the whole surface of the marsh a great cloud of birds hung screaming and circling in the air. I judged at once that some of my shipmates must be drawing near along the borders of the fen. Nor was I deceived, for soon I heard the distant low tones of a human voice, which, as I continued to give ear, grew steadily louder and nearer.

▶ Please continue to the following page

Comprehension

This put me in a great fear, and I crawled under cover of the nearest live-oak and squatted there, hearkening, as silent as a mouse. Another voice answered, and then the first voice, which I now recognized to be Silver's, once more took up the story and ran on for a long while. I drew as close as I could manage, under the favourable ambush of the crouching trees.

Crawling on all fours, I made steadily but slowly towards them. At last, raising my head to an aperture among the leaves, I could see clear down into a little green dell beside the marsh, closely set about with trees. There Long John Silver and another of the crew stood face to face in conversation.

Abridged from Treasure Island, by Robert Louis Stevenson

---

1 What was the narrator feeling at the start of the passage?
- **A** He was pleased because he had pushed Long John down a slippery slope to give himself time to get away.
- **B** He was delighted because he was in unfamiliar territory and he enjoyed exploring.
- **C** Escaping from Long John raised his spirits so that he could take pleasure in other things.
- **D** He was concerned that he was in a strange area, but was hoping to meet new friends.

2 What is meant by the word "tract" in this passage?
- **A** An essay on the subject of flora and fauna of islands
- **B** Dents in the mud and displaced plant life indicating the path of previous walkers
- **C** A poorly constructed lane for horses and people to pass through the forest
- **D** An expanse of land, with no indication of its intended use

▶ Please continue to the following page

Comprehension

3 What did he encounter as he crossed the marshy tract?

- **A** There were bizarre-looking trees.
- **B** Amongst the foliage there were wild animals in constant movement.
- **C** Thick walls of willow that forced him to take a detour
- **D** Here and there, pieces of open sandy country

4 What was the mile-long sandy area like?

- **A** Composed of numerous gentle hills
- **B** Littered with discarded clothing
- **C** Watery and illuminated by the twilight
- **D** Almost impassable because of distorted, pale, trees resembling pines or willows

5 What was his interaction with the rattlesnake?

- **A** It surged at him from the undergrowth and he skirted around it.
- **B** He did not recognise it as a rattlesnake when his path crossed its resting place.
- **C** The sound of the rattlesnake filled him with dread long before he saw it.
- **D** Rising up and spinning out from a rocky ledge, it drove him deeper into the forest.

6 In the third paragraph, what does the narrator think about the island?

- **A** Since he had killed many people on the ship, there should be nobody alive on the island.
- **B** Only unintelligent, thuggish or dishonest people could have got ahead of him.
- **C** The island ahead contained only birds and animals.
- **D** He was terrified when he heard a rattlesnake.

7 What does the narrator say about the evergreen oaks?

- **A** The leaves were widely spread out, admitting shafts of hazy sunlight.
- **B** The branches had notable shapes.
- **C** There was a curiously large amount of sand in the leaves, even in the tall trees.
- **D** Natives of the island had used the leaves to thatch their roofs.

▶ Please continue to the following page

Comprehension

8 Which of these is a true statement about the thicket?

- **A** The tallest trees were in the narrowest part.
- **B** It was surrounded on all sides by a marsh of reeds.
- **C** Some of its shortest trees were on a hill.
- **D** It grew up to the edge of a river, in which he could see an old anchor.

9 What does the narrator say about Spyglass Hill?

- **A** The very warm air was distorting the appearance of the hill.
- **B** The thundering feet of his numerous pursuers were making the outline of the hill tremble.
- **C** Through the steam rising from the marsh it was almost impossible to make out the hill.
- **D** Although they were small, its rivers were so numerous as to almost obscure it from view.

10 What was the narrator doing when squatting under the live-oak?

- **A** Putting all his effort into controlling his fear
- **B** Resisting the temptation to reply
- **C** Avoiding breathing if possible
- **D** Concentrating on listening

11 Which of the following is closest to the meaning of the word "dell" as it is used by the narrator?

- **A** A small dip in the land surrounded by trees
- **B** A boat made from natural products including wood
- **C** An ivy-covered wooden hut in a small valley
- **D** A grassy hill bearing a small stream

12 What was the narrator doing while Silver "took up the story and ran on for a long while"?

- **A** Planning a way to get close and ambush Silver unexpectedly.
- **B** Sketching the layout of the pirates' meeting place as accurately as he could.
- **C** Calculating how to separate the four pirates to make a surprise attack most effective.
- **D** Using natural cover to prevent his discovery while being within earshot.

This is the end of this section. If time remains, check your answers in this section only.

Find the Missing Words

Find the Missing Words

In each of the following sentences, one or two words are missing. Complete the sentence by choosing one word from the choices A to E. Mark your answer on the answer sheet.

You have 4 minutes to answer the questions in this section.

Example

A	B	C	D	E
table	divide	moon	sensible	tube

That night, a bright full [Example] lit their path as they sneaked back into the forbidden garden.

The correct answer is C. Mark it as shown below.

Question 1

A	B	C	D	E
sorry	no	some	much	many

I would like to be able to give you change for the parking meter, but unfortunately I don't have [Question 1] coins.

Question 2

A	B	C	D	E
averse	avarice	abhors	adverse	avers

Many local people were reluctant to join the search party because of [Question 2] weather which had likely contributed to the plane crash.

▶ Please continue to the following page

Find the Missing Words

Paper **H** Page **12**

Question 3

A	B	C	D	E
weeks'	week's	weeks	week	week's'

The exam is in two [Question **3**] time, so we should concentrate on practising.

Question 4

A	B	C	D	E
army	personnel	military	personal	person

It was a mistake to press the button labelled "Do Not Press", we realised, as the air filled with the thud of boots and the room was filled with armed security [Question **4**].

Questions 5 and 6

A	B	C	D	E
complete	complement	complaint	compliment	compliant

"Thank you for being [Question **5**] with our no-smoking rule," said the guide. "The smoke-free atmosphere is a perfect [Question **6**] to the clean, unornamented design of this museum."

Questions 7 and 8

A	B	C	D	E
tick	empathise	tic	sympathise	kindhearted

"I [Question **7**] with that poor boy, twitching away in fear," said the talent show judge (who had never suffered from such trouble) as she awarded him an extra mark for persevering despite his nervous [Question **8**].

❌ **This is the end of this section. If time remains, check your answers in this section only.**

Numerical Reasoning

Numerical Reasoning

On each page there are questions whose answers are numbers, given in the table at the top of the page. For each question, choose the letter A to J which represents the correct answer. Mark your answer on the answer sheet.

You have 11 minutes to answer the questions in this section.

A	B	C	D	E	F	G	H	I	J
12	15	20	24	50	60	108	200	280	320

For the school fair, the children decide to make 5 litres of lemonade. Their recipe for 1 litre of lemonade states to use 3 lemons, 140 g of caster sugar, and top up with water. They have already obtained a half-kilogram bag of caster sugar.

Note:	1 kg = 1000 g	1 kilogram = 1000 grams
	1 l = 1000 ml	1 litre = 1000 millilitres

1. How many lemons will they need in total?
2. How many *more* grams of caster sugar will they need to obtain?
3. If they sell lemonade in portions of 250 ml, how many portions will they have made?

4. A hairdresser has 4 female clients for every male client. How many percent are male?
5. There were sixteen female clients today: how many clients were there altogether?
6. Her fees average £15 for women and £10 for men. What were her total fees today?

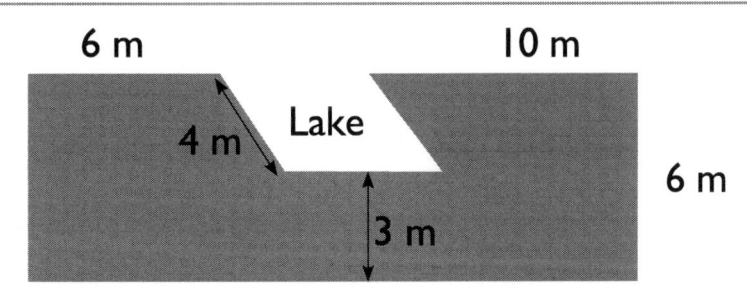

Ivan's garden has at one side a lake shaped like a rhombus (diamond), as shown on this sketch, which is a view from above. Only the grey area, therefore, is covered in grass.

7. The garden is 6 metres wide. How many metres long is it?
8. How many m² is the area of the grass?
9. How many metres is the perimeter of the grass area (shaded in grey)?

▶ Please continue to the following page

Numerical Reasoning

A	B	C	D	E	F	G	H	I	J
1/2	2/3	3/4	3/5	5/6	5/9	0.02	0.25	0.55	0.95

Lucrezia throws a 12-sided die, with sides numbered 1 to 12.

10 What is the chance she throws an even number?

11 What is the chance she throws a number less than 9?

12 If she throws the die twice, what is the chance that both throws are odd?

Six friends played football on various dates, and agreed to pay a share of the £150 rental bill for the year in proportion to how many days they played.

Arthur and Barney attended on all 12 dates. Charles and David only attended 10. Eric came to 5 and Frank to only 1.

13 How large should David's bill be in as a proportion of Barney's?

14 What proportion of the bill should Frank pay?

15 Arthur is short of cash and offers only £20. What proportion of his share is this?

On the EuroStun undersea train to Paris, the cost of a sachet of ketchup, in Euros, is €0.90.

16 If €1.20 is equivalent to £1, what is the price of the ketchup in £?

17 I use a €10 note to buy a coffee for €6.20 and four peanuts for €0.80 each, realising that under the ocean there is nowhere else to go. How much change do I receive, in €?

18 The train company offers me an upgrade to first class, which is normally €192, for the bargain price of €144. What is the discount they are offering me, expressed as a proportion?

✗ This is the end of this section. If time remains, check your answers in this section only.

Similar Words

Paper H Page 15

Similar Words

Identify which word is MOST SIMILAR in meaning to the word on the left.

Each question has only one correct answer. For each question shade your one chosen answer on the answer sheet.

You have 7 minutes to answer the questions in this section.

1 diligent

A	B	C	D	E
water	thin	careful	helpful	clean

2 infamy

A	B	C	D	E
notoriety	homely	unknown	ignorance	information

3 feral

A	B	C	D	E
wild	government	dangerous	metallic	anxious

4 predilection

A	B	C	D	E
suddenness	preference	soothsaying	decreasing	diversion

5 summon

A	B	C	D	E
shared	many	total	frequent	invite

▶ Please continue to the following page

Similar Words

		A	B	C	D	E
6	nuance	softness	never	untried	subtlety	uniqueness

		A	B	C	D	E
7	burgeon	flourish	attack	doctor	request	meal

		A	B	C	D	E
8	vanguard	golden	lock	bumper	vanadium	lead

		A	B	C	D	E
9	dour	flap	acidic	entrance	stern	smell

		A	B	C	D	E
10	prosperity	foresee	affluence	conclusion	magic	ownership

		A	B	C	D	E
11	derive	obtain	propel	conduct	control	flow

		A	B	C	D	E
12	serial	grave	breakfast	sequential	simulated	antenna

		A	B	C	D	E
13	stilted	tall	diagonal	pointed	taken	unnatural

▶ Please continue to the following page

Similar Words

		A	B	C	D	E
14	nag	condone	cherish	connote	criticise	crescent

		A	B	C	D	E
15	synthesise	speculate	make	artistry	decrease	misplace

		A	B	C	D	E
16	exploit	dismantle	expand	trickery	transmit	utilise

		A	B	C	D	E
17	opportune	wealth	miniaturised	convenient	musical	unwrap

		A	B	C	D	E
18	thriving	flourishing	stingy	noisy	painful	remaining

		A	B	C	D	E
19	tantalise	taste	tease	upset	object	oversee

		A	B	C	D	E
20	musing	painting	singing	omitting	considering	utilising

✕ This is the end of this test. If time remains, check your answers in this section only.

Answers to Paper E

Non-Verbal Reasoning

1. **B** In each row, from left to right an extra piece of the background structure is added, identical to the first, either inverted or the correct way up and touching the first. In each column, the number of particles doubles with each step down.

2. **D** In each column, the design rotates clockwise from top to bottom. In each row, the shapes remain unmoved but the colour scheme rotates clockwise from left to right.

3. **A** In each row, the star reflects left to right from one panel to the next. The small round element moves position by one point of the star clockwise, alternating between being in front of the star and behind.

4. **C** In each panel, there are two large shapes that divide the panel into three zones: outside the outer shape, between the shapes, and inside the inner shape. In the left panel, each zone contains one or more small elements. In the middle panel, whatever was in the outer zone moves to the middle zone; whatever was in the middle zone moves to the inner zone; and whatever was in the inner zone moves to the outer zone. This process happens again in the formation of the right panel.

5. **A** The outer element of each of the four corner tiles is rotated right to make the outer element of the corresponding edge tile one position clockwise. The inner elements increase in number within each column from 1 at the top to 3 at the bottom.

6. **A** Within each row, from left to right, the number of bends in the main curve increases by 1. Within each column, the arrow crosses the main curve once in the top cell, twice in the middle cell and three times in the lower cell.

7. **F** In each row, the element in the right cell appears twice in miniature in the middle cell (rotated left and rotated right), together with another small element, and within a large element. The element in the left cell is not related to the other two cells.

8. **C** As your eye passes clockwise, the grey square moves anticlockwise and the arrow moves clockwise (rotating when it reaches a corner). Meanwhile the grey disc moves anticlockwise.

9. **F** The central item is consistent along one diagonal (from bottom left to top right). Around it, rotating clockwise within each column, is another item.

10. **C** The outer element is consistent for each row. For each column, the inner element rotates clockwise 45 degrees in each step from top to bottom.

Numerical Reasoning Part A

Numerical Reasoning Part A

1. **D** Each child's share is 231÷7 = 33. Three children's share totals 33×3 = 99.
2. **B** 70÷4 = 17 remainder 2. He will not have enough after 17 weeks: he needs 18.
3. **E** They are, respectively, £33 1/3, £30, £27, £33, and £32. Arranged in order of size, £32 would be in the middle (median).
4. **B** 17×3 = 51. 51−39 = 12.
5. **E** To midnight it is 1h 30m; after that it is 6h 15m more. Total is therefore 7h 45m.
6. **A** 310 ÷ (7 3/4) = 310 ÷ (31/4) = 310 × 4/31 = 10 x 4 = 40 km/hour.
7. **E** 125 were men. 40%, i.e. 4/10×250 = 4×25 = 100, bought popcorn. The lowest number of men buying popcorn would be 0, if the 100 popcorn buyers were all women. The highest would be 100, if they were all men.
8. **C** Tip: To calculate this efficiently and accurately without having to write out detailed multiplication or division, remember to cancel. The box is 40/100 of 450g = 4/10×450 = 4×45 = 2×90 = 180.
9. **C** 180/2000 = 90/1000 = 9/100 = 9%.
10. **A** Separately, they would cost 5×£0.99 = £4.95. The saving is £4.95 − £3 = £1.95.

Numerical Reasoning Part B

1. **06** Along the bottom, the 9 m outer border is 2 m longer than the 7 m inside border. Since the margin is the same all the way round, the outer border at the sides must be longer by the same amount, 2 m, and must therefore have height 4+2 = 6 m. (Write "0" and "6").
2. **30** The quick way to calculate the perimeter of a rectangle is to add the two different sides and then double the result: (9+6)×2 = 15×2 = 30 m.
3. **26** You could break the grey area into four rectangles, calculate the area of each, and then add them up, but this involves four multiplications and is therefore prone to error. This question is more easily answered by calculating the outer area and subtracting the inner area. Shaded area = 9×6 − 7×4 = 54 − 28 = 26 m^2.
4. **63** Zebras + giraffes must bring the total up to 120, so their total number is 120−(32+12+13) = 120−57 = 63.
5. **42** This is made up of giraffes 2 parts + zebra 1 part. To find out how many is 1 part, divide 63 by the total number of parts (3): 63÷3 = 21. Giraffes are 2 parts, i.e. 2×21 = 42.
6. **41** Decide whether to use kg or g. Using g would give huge numbers (such as 500,000 g), so try kg. Per day, feed eaten by whole flock = 15 × 0.8 kg = 12 kg. Days lasted = 500÷12 = 250/6 = 125/3 (if you cancel like this, the division becomes less error-prone) = 41 2/3.
7. **45** Average = (50+40)÷2=90÷2 = 45.
8. **10** Difference = 30−20 =10.
9. **50** Tabitha increases her score from 30 to 60, i.e. by +30. Griselda starts at 20, and will

therefore (if this happens) finish with 20+30 = 50.

10 **72** 24 × £3 = £72.

11 **90** 6 × £10 + 6 × £5 = £90.

12 **78** Profit on phone chargers = (£5 − £3) × 24 = 2×24 = £48. Profit on scarves = (£10−£5) × 6 = 5 × 6 = £30. Total 48 + 30 = £78.

13 **92** The vertical segments add up to 16 m on the left half of the diagram, and another 16 m on the right half, totalling 32 m. There are horizontals at 6 levels. The topmost is 10m. The next is in two parts totalling 10−2 = 8. The third is 6+6 =12 m. The remainder are mirror images of these, so the total of the horizontal segments is 2×(10+8+12) = 2×30 = 60 m. Total = 32 + 60 = 92 m.

Similar Words

1	D	Dexterity is skill or expertise in performing a physical task, especially using hands.
2	B	Several words have the same general sense, only reported is in the right tense.
3	E	Loot means to steal during a time of public commotion, such as a storm or riot.
4	A	Eloquent means stated in an elaborate, impressive and persuasive manner.
5	D	A member is part of a group or team. (It can also mean arm or leg.)
6	E	Folk means people.
7	C	Semblance means outward or superficial appearance; veneer.
8	E	A staff is a rod or pole used for walking, giving signals, or fighting.
9	B	A chevron is a V-shaped line that functions as an arrow. Examples are: >, <, V, ^.
10	D	To blush is to turn red in the face, especially when shy, embarrassed or ashamed.
11	C	A stony surface is rocky or rugged; a stony person is unfeeling or unsympathetic.
12	E	Upended means tipped upside down, or in a diving position with the head down.
13	B	A rapier is a special light sword with a fine blade used, for example, in fencing.
14	E	A slip can be a fall after sliding, an error, or a piece of paper.
15	C	To elongate is to make something longer, for example by stretching it.
16	D	To quench is to satisfy a thirst by drinking, or put out a fire using water.
17	B	Melodramatic means exaggerated or over-emotional; showy.
18	A	Supreme and paramount mean the greatest, highest ranked or most important.
19	B	To isolate is to cut someone or something off from other people or things.
20	E	A spike is a sudden, large increase in something, or thin, sharp, hard object.
21	D	To accommodate a person can mean allow them a space to live, i.e. house them.
22	B	To entertain a concept is to consider it. To entertain people is to amuse them.

Find the Missing Words

23	A	A granule is a small grain or particle of a substance, for example of salt.
24	D	Previous means in the past. Precious means expensive. A grievous crime is severe.
25	E	Nobility means of good character, or grandeur from being born into aristocracy.
26	B	To glean is to gather information with difficulty from various sources.
27	D	To drench is to soak.

Find the Missing Words

1	B	Coarse means thick or unrefined.
2	D	An aircraft is stored in a hangar, while clothes hang on a hanger.
3	B	Lore means the accumulated knowledge or beliefs held by a group about a subject
4	B	Alter means change, while an altar is a table in a church.
5	C	Counsel is advice or to advise.
6	E	Cancel is to decide or announce that an event won't happen, or to neutralise the effect of something. A council is a group of people.
7	C	In vain means unsuccessfully, a vein is a blood vessel, and a vane indicates wind direction.
8	B	Envelope is a noun. Envelop is a verb meaning to surround.
9	D	It is a meeting for many parents, and therefore it is parents'. If it was for one parent, it would be parent's.
10	C	Accept is to receive something. Aspect means appearance. Except means other than. To expect is to think something will happen.
11	A	To affect is to change something, whereas to effect is to do something. Perhaps confusingly, the change achieved when you affect something is called the effect.
12	A	Thorough means complete and careful.
13	C	A complaint is a statement that something is unsatisfactory. If you are compliant, however, means you tend to agree with the suggestions of others, perhaps excessively.
14	D	A compliment is a positive remark about someone. A complement is something that makes something complete (i.e. fills in a gap).
15	A	To corral is to bring together animals (or people that are wandering aimlessly) into a particular place. Coral is the hard structure at the bottom of the sea, made from animal skeletons.
16	E	Choral means relating to a choir. A chorale is a song for a choir, or a word for the choir itself.

Answers to Paper F

Analogies

1. **D** Although a getaway, capture and a penalty can all follow a crime, it is the penalty that corresponds most closely to how a reward is the consequence of an achievement.
2. **D** A newspaper is consumed by being read. Similarly, a sandwich is consumed by being eaten.
3. **A** Sweden is a country (not a city) in Europe; therefore you must choose a country in Asia, of which only Japan is available.
4. **E** Many is a slightly weaker form of all. Similarly, rarely is a weaker form of never. Many/all relate to proportions of items, while rarely/never relate to how often something happens.
5. **C** An architect builds skyscrapers (in the plural), indicating it is not a single item but a habit of making many items fitting the description. Therefore you must choose something that could be multiple items, i.e. Art, which can apply to multiple statues. **Tip:** When more than one option seems to fit, look carefully at singular versus plural.
6. **D** Cold is a more intense form of cool. Similarly, only ancient is an intensification of old.
7. **E** The process of giving a gift is called presenting. The process of telling a secret is called confiding.
8. **B** A hospital is for the benefit of patients, and a museum is for the benefit of visitors.
   Tip: When the most obvious link, e.g. "hospital contains patients", leads to several options seeming to fit, look for a more specific link.

Shuffled sentences

1. **D** One cannot miss what one has never had.
2. **E** A moment's reflection can save a lifetime of regret.
3. **A** They danced through the night until daybreak.
4. **A** In a land far away, the king lies dying.
5. **B** They say that what goes up must come down.
6. **C** Please invite both of us to your wonderful birthday party.
7. **E** Finally face to face with the monster, George began to tremble. (Or vice versa!)
8. **E** A low rumbling was the only sign that the dam was about to burst. (Or other orders)

Comprehension

Numerical Reasoning Part A

1	D	The Lost Souls in Hell are being punished by being able to see Filboid Studge but not quite being able to reach it.
2	B	Some of the depicted figures resemble famous people of the day.
3	C	Fiends held it in transparent bowls.
4	B	Aviator means aeroplane pilot.
5	C	"… no fulsome allusions to the merits…" Fulsome means excessive or enthusiastic.
6	C	"People will do things from a sense of duty which they would never attempt as a pleasure," and "… would explain in all sincerity that a doctor had ordered them …" Sincerity means they would not be attempting to deceive.
7	A	Austerity means severity or sternness of manner.
8	C	Prefaced means preceded.
9	B	Ostentatious means done in a manner to attract attention and impress others.
10	C	To batten means to fasten or grip firmly. The word originates from the practice of nailing objects together using battens (wooden strips).
11	D	Peer is a word for a lord or lady.
12	A	The regiment mutinied (i.e. refused to follow orders) when the new breakfast was adopted, i.e. they refused to eat it. This was not an actual advertisement. Rather, the event became widely known and so acted as an advertisement.
13	A	It is unpalatable, i.e. horrible-tasting, and its supremacy (top-selling status) might be challenged by an even more unpalatable newcomer.
14	C	"Little in the way of" is an idiom for having little of something (not little to obstruct that thing).
15	A	Half the country is either below sea level or <1m above it. (17% refers to the land reclaimed in a particular way, not the total amount that is below sea level).
16	A	To export is to sell or send to other countries. (The 16th century is the one that ends in 1600, so option D is incorrect.)
17	D	The flood stopped the telephone and telegraph systems from working.
18	D	Caught napping means caught unaware or unprepared.
19	C	Oblivious means unaware. To shore up is to strengthen, not go to the beach. Meteorology is the study of weather.
20	B	The 3 million lived in an area on the verge of flooding, i.e. close to being flooded
21	B	They tried valiantly overnight.
22	B	They deliberately manoeuvred the boat into the growing (burgeoning) gap (cavity or breach).
23	C	"In those days" is a form of words used to refer to a previous time and simultaneously indicate that the current status is different.

Numerical Reasoning Part A

Non-verbal Reasoning

Paper F

1   **C**   Two weeks is 14 days. 14 × 15 = (by mental arithmetic) 140 + 70 = 210.

2   **B**   400 m in 2 minutes. In one hour (60 minutes, i.e. 30 times longer), distance would be 400 × 30 = 12000 m = 12 km.

3   **A**   The fraction not speeding is 40% = 4/10 = 2/5. 2/5×55 = 2×11 = 22. Half are dirty, so the number of non-dirty non-speeding cars is 11.

4   **C**   5.4 + (2×0.45) = 5.4 + 0.9 = 6.3 kg

5   **E**   Since the triangle has one angle of 60° and it is symmetrical, it is an equilateral triangle. Therefore the gap between the two free ends of the stand is also 120 cm. The blackboard is therefore 120 cm wide. It is 60 cm tall. Area = 120×60 = 7200 cm^2.

6   **D**   20000÷2200 = 200/22 = 100/11 = 9 1/11. Nine trips is nearly enough but not actually enough, so he will need to make 10 trips.

7   **D**   Speed = distance ÷ time = 77 km ÷ 55 min = 7/5 km/min = 7/5×60 km/h = 7×12 km/h = 84 km/h.

8   **A**   Time = distance ÷ speed = 77÷44 = 7/4 = 1 3/4 hour = 1 hour 45 min. 11:13 + 01:45 = 12:58. This is after noon (12:00) and therefore in the 12 hour clock it is shown as p.m.

Non-verbal Reasoning

1,2   **B,A**   There are three rings. Their position can be detected because each has varying line thickness around its circumference. The inner ring is rotating clockwise 90°. The outer ring is rotating anticlockwise slower (45°). The intermediate ring is not rotating.

3,4   **C,D**   The arrows are alternating in direction. The small black-and-white square is moving clockwise but its orientation is rotating anticlockwise. The small curve is moving right.

5,6   **D,A**   The triangle is rotating clockwise. Carried with it are one line crossing one side and a pair of parallel lines crossing another side. These lines are progressively changing direction with respect to the triangle: the single line angling with its outer end nearer the original top of the triangle, and the double lines angling the other way.

7,8   **D,A**   At the top, the disc is keeping still while the square moves right, alternately in front of and behind the disc. At the bottom, the dark bar moves progressively down while the disc moves progressively left; the alternate between front and back position. (The bar should not touch the left of the outer square.)

9,10   **B,D**   The arrow is rotating anticlockwise, one-eighth of a turn on each occasion. The pattern of circles is rotating clockwise each turn, and their shading is moving one position anti-clockwise with every step.

11,12   **F,C**   The black-and-white square is moving around the inside of the outer square anticlockwise, half a side at a time, while rotating about its own axis clockwise. The triangle is moving downwards, rotating anticlockwise and alternating in colour.

13,14   **D,C**   The M, J and P move in a circuit clockwise by one place each step. The R is rotating clockwise in orientation.

Numerical Reasoning Part B

15,16   **C,B**   A group of lines is being built up step by step, and there is a diamond falling, alternating in colour.

For a step-by-step training programme in non-verbal reasoning with *graphical explanations* and systematically covering numerous modern question types, take the 3-part ***Non-Verbal Ninja* Training Course**.

Numerical Reasoning Part B

1. **15**   1 litre/second = 3600 litres per hour. Volume to fill = 3/4 × 72,000 = 54,000 L. Time = 54,000÷3,600 = 540/36 = (cancelling by 2) 270/18 = (cancelling by 9) 30/2 = 15. **Tip**: you may at first have calculated 54000÷3600 by long division, but it is sometimes easier to avoid mistakes if you cancel first. (*Eureka! Maths and Numerical Reasoning* books give more advice on making difficult questions easy.)

2. **64**   White or black: 8+24=32. Total number of socks = 50. Percentage = 32/50×100 = 32×2 = 64%.

3. **54**   **Tip**: When tiling a rectangle, it sometimes avoids decimals or very large numbers to immediately calculate how many tiles fit along its length and breadth.

   Answer: Tiles along length = 9/0.5 = 18. Tiles along width = 1.5/0.5 = 3. Total number of tiles = 18 × 3 = 54.

4. **41**   The angle adjacent to 131° is 180−131 = 49°. Since the angles inside a triangle must add up to 180° and 90° is already accounted for in the right angle at the bottom, what remains, 49 + a, must add up to 90. Therefore a = 90−49 = 41.

5. **81** $(6+3)^2 = 9^2 = 81$.

6. **13** $(q+7)^2 = 400$ means q+7 = 20, so q =13.

7. **18**   3% of £600: 1% is £6, so 3% is £18.

8. **56**   There are 8 short straight sides of 3 m, totalling 8×3 = 24 m. There are 4 curved sides, totalling 4×8 = 32 m. Perimeter = 24 + 32 = 56 m.

Answers to Paper G

Numerical Reasoning

1. **C** 3/5 $2 \times 0.5 \times 0.6 = 0.6$ m^3.
2. **J** 1/100 $0.2 \times 0.2 \times 0.15 = 0.006$ m^3. This is 1/100 of 0.6 m^3.
3. **G** 1 1/5. $2 \times 0.6 = 1.2$ m^2.
4. **A** 1/2. Half the numbers are even, so the chance is 1/2.
5. **D** 2/3. *More* than two means 3, 4, 5, 6. (2 is not more than 2.) 4/6 = 2/3.
6. **H** 1/36. The only way to score 2 is to score 1 and 1. Chance = 1/6 × 1/6 = 1/36.
7. **B** 1/4. 5+8+7 = 20. 5/20 = 1/4.
8. **C** 3/5. 50−20 dogs = 30 cats. 30/50 = 3/5
9. **A** 1/2. 20 dogs + 20 cats = 40 animals. 20/40 = 1/2.
10. **H** 132. 6.6 cm × 2 million = 13.2 million cm = 0.132 million m = 132 000 m = 132 km.
11. **G** 120. 12.7−10.3 = 2.4 cm. 2.4 × 5 000 = 12 000 cm = 120 m.
12. **I** 400. 2 000 000 ÷ 5000 = 400.
13. **J** 2250. Monthly base salary = £15000÷12 = £1250. 1250 + 2×500 = £2250.
14. **F** 40. She needs to get £35000−£15000 = £20000 from sales. 20 000 ÷ 500 = 40.
15. **F** 40. Extra is 10000. 10000÷25000 = 10/25 = 40/100 = 40%.
16. **E** 36. 6×7=42. 42−6=36.
17. **D** 20. $7n - 6 = 134$, so $7n = 140$, so $n = 20$.
18. **A** 1. $7n - 6 = n$, so $6n = 6$, and $n = 1$.

Non-Verbal Reasoning

Paper **G**

Non-Verbal Reasoning

Answers

1	E
2	E
3	C
4	B
5	D
6	A
7	D
8	F
9	D
10	C
11	C
12	B
13	E

Visual Explanation for Question 1

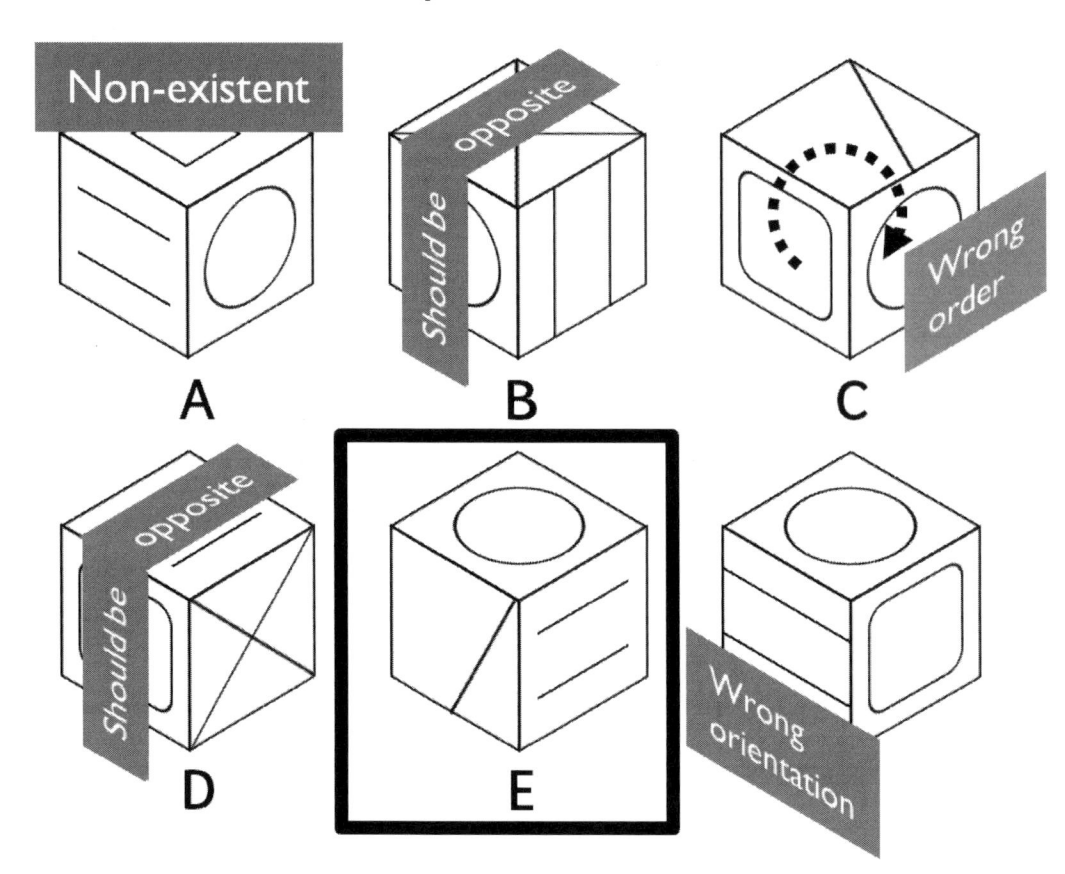

A — Non-existent
B — Should be opposite
C — Wrong order
D — Should be opposite
E — (correct answer)
F — Wrong orientation

Three-dimensional puzzles such as these net-and-cube questions test awareness of position in space, and the ability to mentally rotate elements or an entire picture.

Book 2 of the Non-Verbal Ninja Training Course starts from the basics of 3D puzzles, and builds up to advanced types. It presents a **simple, memorable method** for solving these net-and-cube puzzles consistently.

Like all the books of the Non-Verbal Ninja Training Course, it emphasises **visual** explanations.

Find the Missing Words

Paper **G**

Find the Missing Words

1	C	rhyme	It is a nursery rhyme.
2	E	century	Century best fits a description of a long duration of fame.
3	A	language	For "words" to fit, the next two words would have to be "that do".
4	B	everyday	Everyday helps the sentence indicate familiarity or commonness.
5	E	probe	Probe means enquire or look into.
6	A	represent	Only represent has the right meaning and tense.
7	D	devastated	Only devastated is a verb meaning destroyed and in the right tense.
8	A	population	The text that follows make clear that it was people who were killed.
9	C	ghost	If many people are killed, a small village may look like a ghost town.
10	A	include	Only include has the right meaning in the right tense.
11	C	sneezing	Atishoo is onomatopoeia for sneezing.
12	A	contracted	Contracted means caught (a disease).
13	D	infectious	Infectious indicates that they could pass on the disease.
14	B	ward	Ward off means fend off, push away or keep away.
15	B	However,	The following text suggests the previous text was wrong.
16	D	Before	The next sentence tells us the mentions were common after 1940.
17	A	link	Association would need to be preceded by "an".
18	E	dominant	Only dominant conveys the meaning of leading, and fits.
19	C	never	Speculate and theorise could only fit if the word "learn" was not there.
20	B	events	People or pestilences might have fitted, but not person or pestilential.
21	A	emerged	Surfaced, come or been remembered would fit, but were not offered.
22	D	how	If true, someone would have noted how it was discovered.
23	B	possible	The text does not say that the plague explanation is certainly wrong.

Groups

Paper G

Groups

1	**B**	A rucksack is an example of luggage.
2	**D**	Lead, the element, is an example of material.
3	**A**	Truncation means shortening, especially by chopping off the end.
4	**E**	An amphibian is a creature that lives on land and in water, such as a frog.
5	**A**	An arrow is an example of a pointer.
6	**D**	A console is an example of equipment.
7	**B**	A reflection is a common example of an image. Reputation is a synonym for another meaning of the word image, but is not an example of it.
8	**B**	A runner is an athlete.
9	**A**	Khaki is a light shade of brown, commonly used in military uniforms.
10	**C**	A slice is an example of the general principle of a segment.
11	**B**	A leotard is an example of a costume, used in dancing or gymnastics.
12	**D**	Spring (noun) is an example of season (which).
13	**A**	A chasm is a particular type (very large) of gap.
14	**B**	Rapids are fast-flowing, turbulent segments of rivers.
15	**E**	To point is one way to indicate.
16	**D**	A glut is an excessively abundant quantity.
17	**A**	A conclusion is a decision or judgement stated after a process of reasoning.
18	**A**	To mould is to reshape. A scaling, in general, does not change shape.
19	**A**	Berlin is the capital of Germany.
20	**C**	To raffle is one way to allocate items.
21	**E**	A diamond is one example of a shape.
22	**A**	A condiment is a flavouring that is added to food by a diner shortly before eating.
23	**B**	A salve is an ointment placed on the skin to soothe or heal it.
24	**D**	Quadruped means creature with four legs.
25	**A**	My ancestor is anyone from whom I am descended: a parent's parent's ... parent.
26	**C**	Of the options available, an itch is the best example of a specific irritation.
27	**E**	A pipe organ is a type of organ, but a pipe is not an organ. The liver is an organ.
28	**B**	An amethyst is a precious stone. A weight is not an example of a stone.

Answers to Paper H

Shuffled sentences

1. **C** There is no substitute for hard work.
2. **C** At last he emerged from the cave into the bright summer sun.
3. **B** Cakes and biscuits were his favourite foods despite being unhealthy. (Or other orders)
4. **C** After a grand drum roll the magician revealed the contents of the hat.
5. **A** The order to begin was considerably delayed.
6. **D** Stall your brother while I finish wrapping his present.
7. **D** A Polish friend sent us a silver spoon.
   (Note that capitalisation of words is not necessarily correct in the shuffled sentence.)
8. **B** As the tears well up, he reaches for a tissue.

Non-verbal Reasoning

1. **E** In the middle row, each panel is composed of the combination of the contents of the corresponding panels in the top and bottom rows.
2. **C** Each panel is composed of three elements: top (located at top-right), middle, and bottom (located at bottom left). The top elements are consistent within each row; the bottom elements are consistent within each column. The middle elements are consistent in shape within each row but alternate in direction.
3. **C** In each row, the design in the left panel is replicated in all 4 rotational positions within the outer square, as is the design in the middle panel, to make the right panel.
4. **F** In each column, the outer shape becomes taller and narrower from top to bottom. In each row, the inner shape rotates clockwise very slightly from left to right.
5. **E** In each row the number of large outline shapes increases by one from left to right. In each column the number of small shaded discs increases by one from top to bottom. The small shaded discs are always in the area where all the outline shapes overlap.
6. **D** In each row, the element on the left, duplicated with an 180 degree rotation, plus the element in the middle, also duplicated with an 180 degree rotation, gives the element on the right.

Comprehension

Paper H

7	F	The number of elements in the right column is always the number in the left column, minus the number in the middle column.
8	B	The elements in middle and bottom cells of each column are combined, and then duplicated by reflection in the vertical midline, to make the top cell.
9	D	For each row, the total number of elements in the left and middle panels is the number of sides of the shape in the right panel.

Comprehension

1	C	It was because he had given John the slip (i.e. escaped) that he could enjoy other things.
2	D	A tract is an expanse of land, usually large.
3	A	Outlandish means bizarre.
4	A	Undulating means wave-like or gently hilly.
5	B	It did rise up but it was the sound that resembled a spinning top. He didn't recognise it.
6	C	Dumb brutes means unspeaking animals; fowl means birds.
7	B	The boughs (which means branches) were curiously twisted.
8	C	It "spread down from one of the knolls (hills) … growing taller as it went".
9	A	The strong sun heated the air, making objects viewed through it seem to shimmer.
10	D	Hearkening (also spelled harkening) is listening.
11	A	A dell is a small valley, most often surrounded by trees.
12	D	The ambush from the crouching trees is a metaphor: they are surrounding him, providing convenient natural cover.

Find the Missing Words

1	E	Much is used with singular nouns, such as hair, water, time, money, work, and help. Many is used with plural nouns.
2	D	Averse means having a dislike of something. Adverse means obstructive, unfavourable or harmful. Avers means states emphatically that something is true.
3	A	It is a time of two weeks, which is why we write "weeks' time".
4	B	Personnel is a noun for a group of staff. Personal is an adjective, meaning private or relating to one individual.
5	E	Compliant means obedient, while complaint means objection or statement that something is unsatisfactory.

Numerical Reasoning

Paper H

6   **B**   A complement means a suitable fit, for example between two pieces in a jigsaw. A compliment is praise.

7   **D**   You can empathise with someone going through the same emotions as you did in the past, most commonly because you had the same experience.

            You can sympathise with anyone if you feel sorrow or pity for their situation: there is no need for you to have been in the same situation in the past.

8   **C**   A tic is a habitual twitch, particularly if it occurs in response to anxiety. A tick is a mark drawn to indicate an answer is correct, or a small insect, or the sound of a clock.

Numerical Reasoning

1   **B**   **15**. 5 litres × 3 lemons per litre = 15 lemons.

2   **H**   **200**. 5×140 = 700. 700 − 500 = 200 ml.

3   **C**   **20**. 5000 ml ÷ 250 ml = 500/25 = (cancel by 5) 100/5 = 20.

4   **C**   **20**. 1÷(4+1) = 1/5 = 20%.

5   **C**   **20**. 80% of N is 16, so 10% of N is 2, and 100% of N is 20.

6   **I**   **280**. 15×16 + 10×4 = 240+40 = 280.

7   **C**   **20**. Because the lake is a rhombus, its four sides are equal, 4m. 6+4+10=20 m.

8   **G**   **108**. Height of rhombus is 6−3 = 3 m. 20×6 − 4×3 = 120−12 =108 m.

9   **F**   **60**. Full rectangle would be 2×(20+6) = 52. Add two *extra* rhombus sides (8): 60.

10   **A**   **1/2**. Half of the sides are even.

11   **B**   **2/3**. There are 8 values less than 9. (Nine is not less than nine.) 8/12 = 2/3.

12   **H**   **0.25**. Chance of two odd throws = (1/2) × (1/2) = 1/4.

13   **E**   **5/6**. He attended 10 versus 12 for Barney. 10/12 = 5/6

14   **G**   **0.02**. 12+12+10+10+5+1=50 attendances. Each attendance is worth 1/50th

15   **F**   **5/9**. Arthur should pay 12/50 × £150 = 12×3 = £36. 20/36 = 5/9.

16   **C**   **3/4**. €0.90 is 3/4 of €1.20, so it is 3/4 of £1.

17   **D**   **3/5**. €6.20+4×€0.80 = €9.40. Change = €0.60. This is 3/5 of a €.

18   **H**   **0.25**. Discount = 192−144 = 48. As a proportion, this is 48/192. Both top and bottom are multiples of 12, so it can be simplified to 4/16 = 1/4 = 0.25.

Similar Words

Similar Words

1	**C**	Diligent means showing care in one's work.
2	**A**	Infamy is being famous for a bad feature.
3	**A**	Feral means wild or seeming to be wild.
4	**B**	Predilection means preference.
5	**E**	Summon means order or invite someone to come somewhere.
6	**D**	A nuance is a subtle difference in or shade of meaning.
7	**A**	Burgeon means grow or flourish, and be increasing in size or importance.
8	**E**	The vanguard is the front part of an army or group: the part that leads the way. Vanadium is a metal.
9	**D**	Dour means severe, stern or lacking in enthusiasm.
10	**B**	Prosperity is the state of being financially successful or gaining material wealth.
11	**A**	To derive is to obtain something by a particular method or from a particular place.
12	**C**	Serial means repeated episodes, for example, a serial killer or a television serial.
13	**E**	Stilted speech or writing is stiff and unnatural; excessively formal.
14	**D**	To nag is to repeatedly criticise, remind, harass, or make request of someone.
15	**B**	To synthesise is to make something.
16	**E**	To exploit is to use fully, and derive the full potential benefit from.
17	**C**	Opportune, of a moment in time, means appropriate, convenient or fortunate.
18	**A**	Thriving means being successful, growing, flourishing.
19	**B**	To tantalise is to tease or attract someone with an exciting possibility.
20	**D**	Musing means considering or thinking about something for some time.

Verbal Reasoning: The 1000 Word Brain Boost Advanced Training Workbooks

The *1000-Word Brain Boost* is a powerful, intensive course teaching Synonyms, Antonyms, Odd-One-Out, Analogy, Vocabulary and Cloze in CEM-style questions. Its famous *Explanations* section explains hundreds of language subtleties and distinctions that many 11+ candidates find challenging.

21816415R00052

Printed in Great Britain
by Amazon